EYES
BEYOND
THE
HORIZON

EYES
BEYOND
THE
HORIZON

$$\longleftrightarrow$$

ELEANOR G. BOWMAN
WITH SUSAN F. TITUS

Published in Nashville, Tennessee, by Thomas Nelson, Inc., and distributed in Canada by Lawson Falle, Ltd., Cambridge, Ontario.

Unless otherwise noted, Scripture quotations are from the NEW KING JAMES VERSION of the Bible. Copyright © 1979, 1980, 1982, Thomas Nelson, Inc., Publishers.

Library of Congress Cataloging-in-Publication Data

Bowman, Eleanor G.
  Eyes beyond the horizon / Eleanor G. Bowman with Susan F. Titus.
    p. cm.
  ISBN 0-8407-7235-1 (pbk.)
  1. Far East Broadcasting Company. 2. Radio in religion.
  3. Bowman, Robert H. (Robert Henry), 1915–   4. Bowman, Eleanor G.
I. Titus, Susan F. II. Title.
BV656.B68   1991
269'.26'0601—dc20
                                                            90–41338
                                                               CIP

Printed in the United States of America
1 2 3 4 5 6 7 — 95 94 93 92 91

Dedication

Far East Broadcasting Company (FEBC) has been one of the most effective and consistent voices in evangelical Christianity in the entire world.

We thank God for every evangelical voice using modern technology to herald the gospel of Jesus Christ.

Dr. Billy Graham

The use of radio as a communications tool in the task of world evangelism over the last fifty years has been the second most powerful breakthrough in the two-thousand-year history of missions. Only printing has taken priority of place.

God has used FEBC to lead the way in this incredible breakthrough.

The miraculous growth of the church in China is attributable in significant measure to gospel broadcasting. Indeed, it is said that over 50 percent of the millions who have turned to faith in Jesus Christ over the past ten years were first touched by gospel broadcasting. Here FEBC has played a major role.

Eyes Beyond the Horizon is the gripping account of the way in which the Risen Lord has used FEBC to embrace the people of the world with the saving gospel of

Jesus Christ. It is also an urgent call to consider the unfinished dimensions of the Great Commission and to
do something about it.

> James Hudson Taylor III
> Singapore
> 21 February 1990

Bob Bowman and Far East Broadcasting Company are
synonymous in my thinking. Bob and Eleanor and FEBC
have made and continue to make a mighty impact for our
Lord throughout the world. To me, FEBC and other similar
ministries are the unsung heroes of our time, having pene-
trated iron and bamboo curtains for decades where it was
unlawful, illegal, and dangerous to use other approaches.
There are few people whom I hold in higher esteem. I give
thanks to our wonderful Lord upon every remembrance of
Bob and Eleanor, two of God's choicest ambassadors.

> Yours for fulfilling the Great
> Commission in this generation,
> William R. Bright
> President
> Campus Crusade for Christ,
> International

I have known of the significant ministries of FEBC
since its earliest days in the Philippines and rejoice in the
magnificent role it has played over the decades in pro-
claiming the good news of the gospel across the world.
Bob and Eleanor Bowman are choice servants of Christ,
and this record of God's faithfulness in pioneering Christian radio is long overdue. I am most pleased to com-

mend it—and FEBC—to any and all. What a testimony
they—and it—have been over these years!

Your Friend in Christ,
Ted W. Engstrom
President Emeritus
World Vision

It was a sad day when all missionaries were ordered
to leave China. They wondered: Could the fragile Church
of less than a million true believers survive? They had
watched as churches were confiscated, Bibles burned,
and pastors sent to prison.

They questioned: Would the Church starve for lack of
spiritual bread? "In the fullness of time," Christ raised up
Far East Broadcasting Company to send spiritual manna to
the hungry of China. For over four decades, this saving,
feeding, and equipping ministry has kept the believers
strong and the church growing. Today, this worldwide
work continues not only in Chinese but in over a hundred
other languages.

FEBC is worthy of sincere prayers and sacrificial support. We feel honored that, in a small way, we can participate in this fruitful ministry.

Dick Hillis
Founder
Overseas Crusades,
Incorporated

Writing this book was an awesome task, and I accepted it reluctantly. FEBC is a four-decade record of God's
direction and the deeds of 854 dedicated full-time FEBC
staff members scattered across the world—90 percent of

whom are nationals of the countries of the broadcasting targets—plus 120 volunteers and hundreds who have served and departed. To keep this book readable thousands of exciting stories were left untold, and the greater majority of the names of those who served and are serving to accomplish this work are omitted.

My husband, Bob Bowman, helped with putting the book together, collaborating on every sensitive detail, and then Susan Titus expertly and professionally fine-tuned it.

Bob is still going strong with the same enthusiasm for the ministry of the Far East Broadcasting Company as the first day it began! His administrative responsibilities have taken him on thousands of trips to Asia, across the United States and Canada, and to far places of the world. When he loses his joy and enthusiasm for the work or some of the excellent health the Lord has blessed him with, he concedes he *may* think of doing something else.

On the go all the time, he doesn't seem to know he's used up his "threescore and ten."

Words in Ecclesiastes 5:20 describe him: "For he will not dwell unduly on the days of his life, because God keeps him busy with the joy of his heart."

He loves each staff member of the widely separated staff. They all welcome his presence. They say, "He is the 'glue' that keeps us all together. We love to have him come and tell us what *we* are doing!"

A Filipino staff member wrote this:

Dr. Robert H. Bowman
President, FEBC Radio International

To you, "Uncle Bob," dearly loved by all of us . . .
A man whose heart is stirred by God . . . in
    passion for the world.

Stirred to give himself unselfishly to touch lives
for God.

Stirred with burning deep desire to reach out till
East and West are caught in God's
all-embracing love.
Stirred by Christ's constraining love to stir others
to be heralds of the day before the curtains of
night fall.

To my husband Bob, the entire staff of the Far East
Broadcasting Company, and those who support this
work of God in prayer and giving, this book is joyfully
dedicated.

Eleanor G. Bowman

Table of Contents

The Joyful Song

"The joyful sound: Jesus saves! Jesus saves!" resounds in more than one hundred languages around the world, beamed from the huge antennas of Far East Broadcasting Company. Daily, FEBC transmits this message of hope through three hundred program hours from radio stations in five widely separated countries. Though only a few people ever see these stations and their tall towers, the announcers' voices are heard by hundreds of millions. Their words embrace the power to give Life to all who hear.

Meanwhile, around the world many people admire the tall steeples of elegant churches and cathedrals. These spires also lift high into the air, reaching toward the heavens in reverence to God. These architectural monuments stand as an ultimate expression of what individuals created by God can offer to Him by the works of their hands. The magnificent steeples raise the eyes of earthbound individuals upward toward God. Their bells ring out over cities and countrysides, calling people to worship and adore their Lord.

Yet perhaps the most commanding spires erected to the glory of God have been raised on far island shores, noticed by few. Gigantic steel towers of thirty-two international AM mediumwave and shortwave radio stations of FEBC ascend from landscapes as diverse as the languages they broadcast.

Steel towers rise from congested, rural barrios on the

outskirts of Manila. Huge antennas lift from the rice paddies of Bocaue, nestle beside a palm-fringed shore in remote Zambales, and soar on a hilltop in Cebu. They spire upward on a jungle clearing on Mindanao, on the outskirts of tension-filled Davao, above the simmering heat of near-equatorial Zamboanga, amid sugar plantations in Bacolod, and under the rumblings of Mayon Volcano in Legaspi.

High on a Saipan cliff, a gigantic antenna array rises 620 feet above the ocean surface. Anchored to coral beds, towers emerge from the waters of the Indian Ocean in the Seychelles. Others stand as sentinels on ancient burial grounds on Cheju-do in the Yellow Sea and on the shoreline of Inchon, minutes away from Korea's demilitarized zone. Still other huge towers rise over the salt flats of San Francisco Bay.

These steel structures offer surpassing beauty to the eyes of those whose vision has been opened by the Spirit to behold the unseen. They radiate vibrant life, singing with electronic energy. The antennas pulsate with the power to fling a message thousands of miles across great seas, over vast land and mountain masses, and into the far reaches of our entire spinning world. The resulting radio waves contact their targets in split seconds.

Far East Broadcasting Company is a unique organization that started with no financial backing, no supportive board, and no church denomination. It began simply in 1945 with two young men named John and Bob who made a quiet commitment to the will of God. Accomplishments never dreamed of are now realities, propelled by the miracle-working hand of God.

1

At Last! At Last! We Occupy the Land!

Not a leaf of the flame trees stirred on Marpi Cliff. Douglas Campbell found the stillness foreboding and unnerving. In the early morning dawn he watched the dark clouds as they formed a circle around the tiny island of Saipan. The menacing clouds hung back on the horizon, brooding, threatening with an evil intent to sweep land and sea into their possession.

The inhabitants of Saipan had gone to bed Tuesday night, December 6, 1986, assured by the weather reports that the tropical storm roaming the Pacific Ocean would pass south of their island. However, Doug was not reassured by the report. He knew the storm had nursed itself into the full fury of Super Typhoon Kim.

Saipan, a seventy-square-mile island of the Northern Marianas, lying in the Pacific Ocean fourteen hundred miles south of Tokyo, had known many typhoons. Others had come near, only to veer off in another direction. The sideswipe alone was awesome. Some had hit the island but not with the strength that Typhoon Kim promised.

Suddenly Doug was startled by the viciousness with which a squall of rain hit the side of his house. He felt that this was no ordinary tropical storm, and he knew that the paths of severe cyclonic disturbances are uncertain. Previous experiences with typhoon warnings gave Doug reason for his uneasiness.

As the newly appointed director of Far East Broadcasting Company's Saipan operation, Doug had responsibility for the powerful overseas broadcasting stations on Marpi Cliff. Outside his window he could see the building that held five transmitters with power totaling one-half million watts and the antennas that increased the effective-radiated signals.

Added to his concern was the safety of the staff. Several families lived on Marpi Cliff. Their homes and his faced the sea, strung out in a wide curve along a slight indenture that dropped off sharply four hundred feet to the sea.

Below, at almost sea level and ten miles south along the shoreline, was KSAI. As well as being Far East Broadcasting Company's local station, it was Saipan's only weather warning station. The people of Saipan, Tinian, and several small outlying islands and atolls of the Northern Marianas chain relied upon it for their weather warnings. For this reason KSAI remained on the air night and day during this critical time.

Doug knew that as Typhoon Kim picked up force, people would tune in for reports. He tried to call the island's alarm preparedness agency, but their phones were down.

Doug dressed quickly and turned to his wife. Their eyes met wordlessly. They both knew what he had to do. When Doug left Karen and their sleeping children, he did not realize that it would be forty-eight hours before they would be together again.

As he drove down the curving white coral road that FEBC had built, he was reminded once again that this was the same dark ravine where the last World War II Japanese banzai charge had taken place on the island. Under the dark overhang of elephant grass and papaya trees, rain blasted against the car. The loud, whistling wind made him more aware of impending calamity.

Upon reaching the Di Con Disaster Center, which picks up relayed weather information from the navy on Guam, he read the latest code. Typhoon Kim had reversed directions and was headed straight for Saipan.

Jumping back into his car, he radioed the report to the staff on Marpi and continued on to KSAI. Gusts of wind attacked with a fury that almost tipped his car over. At the station he joined the senior announcer on duty, and they gave typhoon bulletins to the people.

Besides the twenty-five thousand residents of Saipan, there were one thousand people on Tinian, an island seven miles off shore, and fifteen hundred more on Rota to the south. Also approximately three hundred small islands and atolls with about a hundred inhabitants were strung out 250 miles to the north.

Doug had planned to leave the operator on duty and return to his family on Marpi, but at 7:00 A.M. the real force of Typhoon Kim struck. The two men found themselves pinned down in the concrete station building for the next five hours. The typhoon rampaged across the island at wind speeds of 160 miles per hour.

Torrents of rain poured over the small island as the storm swept the ocean to land. Situated close to the shoreline, KSAI sustained a beating.

This provided quite a contrast with the normal scene. Usually the waves whispered against the sandy beaches. The turquoise and green lagoons inside the coral barrier reefs reflected white clouds against a hot, blue sky. The silky smoothness of the still lagoon also mirrored fiery sunsets and starry night skies.

Yet today, huge gale-driven sea waves crashed over the protective reefs to drown the land. Coconuts, tin roofs, pieces of wood and steel, and uprooted trees whirled around on the deadly wind as though they were toothpicks! The storm held the island hostage as it circled in senseless destruction.

At the height of the storm, after three hours of broadcasting warnings, KSAI's antenna wire broke, and the station went off the air. Two feet of water flooded the building.

Up on Marpi Cliff, FEBC engineers fought against the strong gales to secure property, to pick up tools and equipment, and to bolt heavy storm shutters over all the windows.

Suddenly, with overpowering might, the typhoon exploded all around the exposed buildings on the cliff. It picked up everything that lay in its whirling, screaming path and smashed it against the concrete walls.

The steep coral roadway became a fast-flowing waterfall. The wind and rain took deep bites from the white cliff's limestone edge. The tangin-tangin bushes surrounding the clearing roiled and heaved like angry sea waves.

Inside, the FEBC staff prayed and thanked God for the sturdy buildings. They reassured the children when the increasing blasts ripped the strong shutters from the windows and glass exploded inward. Sheets of horizontally driven water forced its way inside, soaking everything.

Shrill, unearthly shrieks pierced the steady roar that sounded like a dozen jet engines bearing down. The storm raged hour after terrifying hour.

The staff watched the exposed towers with apprehension. The towers had been built to withstand winds up to two hundred miles per hour. Later they learned that the towers withstood 198-mile-per-hour gusts!

The towers held steady, but the heavy wires strung between them eventually snapped. The staff watched in anguish as the components of the beautiful antenna arrays were torn to shreds and left hanging in a tangled mass of wire with a few insulators bobbing crazily between. The transmitters were safe in their protected buildings, but the life-giving transmissions ceased.

Then came a sudden lull—a silence as terrifying as the deafening sound. It seemed as though the storm was holding its breath to gain hateful strength.

The shocking quiet was tense, unnatural, as the air was being sucked out. Encased in the dark counterclockwise vortex of the storm, members of the staff caught startling glimpses of jagged bits of blue sky overhead. Then, after about twenty minutes, the eye of the storm passed. The dreaded sound began to roll back in from a distance like a steadily increasing drumbeat, until it again reached painful decibels. Reversing and expanding, the winds swooped down again with renewed wrath.

Typhoon Kim finally wearied itself with its own exploding violence and wheeled out to sea, leaving the island in unbelievable chaos. People wandered around in shock. Their energy seemed to be wrenched from them. The long stress of the gale left weariness of body, numbness of spirit, and saddened hearts.

Four thousand people on Saipan lost their homes and possessions. The island's power plant sustained damage. Schools were destroyed, businesses were swept away, and roads were under three feet of water. Miraculously only one person had died.

On Marpi Cliff the Far East Broadcasting staff inspected the damage. How thankful they were for the heavy security of the concrete buildings constructed by the crew of volunteers years before. Yet emotionally they felt grief and loss because the antennas hung in shreds. It meant listeners in FEBC's target areas tuned their radios and wondered, "Where did they go?"

Although the roofs were secure, great water damage

took place. Windows were shattered. Paint was scuffed from the buildings. The island's power shut down. The ravine roadway that wound four hundred feet up the Marpi Cliff was gouged by rain and wind, making chuckholes as deep as the shell craters left during World War II.

Doug Campbell immediately reported back to the United States:

> We, as a staff and individually, have faced a disaster. While we're in shock of the effect of the storm on our facilities and what it means to the ministry, we never question for a moment that God is in control. We're not asking God, "Why did this happen?" Although we do wonder why it did happen. We know that God has sent each of us here for His individual reason, and we know that He will glorify Himself through this. He's teaching us things, and we're now asking God, "What is the challenge before us? How can we best meet this challenge? How can You receive glory from this? And Lord, thank You for letting us be here at this time, because You are going to let us participate in meeting the challenge of glorifying Your Name."

> We are having a staff meeting at least once a day, mainly to encourage each other. And in sharing what happened, we talked about needing to release our emotions to each other. We concluded with Psalm 96:3: "Declare His glory among the nations, / His wonders among all peoples." We still sing of God's glory among nations, and that is our theme for rebuilding our lives and our broadcasting site here.

The FEBC Saipaners went to work. FEBC engineers, assisted by Trans World Radio engineers from Guam, reestablished a "fair-weather" central beam to China and central Russia. The northern beam to Siberia, however, was totally destroyed. The beam to Southeast Asia was also lost. The total damage was over $500 thousand.

In America, thousands more became aware of FEBC's ministry as the disaster was reported through secular as well as the Christian media. The faithful supporters of Far East Broadcasting Company responded, as did new friends. Within less than six months, the entire amount needed was in hand, and the necessary repairs were made. The north beam took longer to repair, but with height added to the towers on which it hung, a greater efficiency was gained.

Most importantly, the millions of people who listen to FEBC broadcasts again heard the good news of Christ's gospel, reaching their radios from the repaired antennas on Saipan.

Beginning in 1947 Far East Broadcasting Company began to construct radio stations for sending the gospel to lands that had little or no witness of Christ. After building the first stations in the Philippines, they moved on to build others on Okinawa. They purchased a powerful international station in San Francisco, obtained licenses to build in the Seychelles, and built stations in Korea. Now they restored the antennas on Saipan.

New opportunities to expand seemed to open before the last projects were completed. And only a short time was available to go through the doors of opportunity before they closed, so FEBC pressed forward, "eyes beyond the horizon," seeking the unreached.

Why was Saipan chosen by FEBC as a transmitting site? Saipan became a United States trust territory under the control of the United States at the end of World War II. It was administered by a resident commissioner, Erwin Canham. Through the good graces of his office and the Northern Marianas government, the proper legal papers were eventually obtained for the building of a local radio station, KSAI, to service Saipan and the Northern Marianas. The overseas transmitting objective to China and Southeast Asia came later.

Norman Blake spent three weeks on Saipan the latter part of 1975 filing the application papers. Norman and his wife Mavis moved from the FEBC station on Cheju-do, South Korea, to Saipan in December. Coming from the FEBC station in Iba, Zambales, Philippines, Byrd and Angie Brunemeier joined them. Just as they had in the Philippines, the two families spearheaded the advance into the new territory of Saipan. Several FEBC families joined them. They decided first to place a local station on the air to reach the people of Saipan and neighboring islands. KSAI was built on property close to the waterfront leased to FEBC from a local church organization. This land did not have the space for an antenna system, and it was impossible to put the local station on the air at full power without a proper antenna to radiate the signal.

Two years full of intense work and agonizing reversals passed. One difficulty after another arose. Finally the government granted the franchise. FEBC leased a piece of swampland for the local station, KSAI. Immediately, Byrd and his crew went to work clearing the swamp. They reported that the grading was done in only fourteen days.

But the good news was short lived. Local opposition arose. Although proper legal permits were obtained, FEBC personnel felt obligated as Christians to submit to the governor's request to hold back the activity and look for other land. Byrd said: "I sadly drove the red tractor back to the bodega [warehouse] and put it away. We did not create the problem. We just walked into an historic problem."

Difficulty began during World War II. The Allied forces painfully fought their way through the South Pacific from one small group of islands to another: Tarawa, the Gilberts, right up to the threshold of the Japanese Mandated Islands. Kwajalein, Majuro, and Eniwetok in the Marshall Islands were attacked and taken.

Saipan and Tinian, two of the Marianas islands, became the next target. Thirty thousand Japanese troops were firmly entrenched to defend Saipan, holed up in caves and along strategic cliffs.

On the morning of June 15, 1944, heavy guns of the United States Navy ships laid down an overpowering barrage from one end of the island to the other. The defenders had placed guns on ridges running parallel to the water landing areas, sweeping the reef. Nevertheless, by day's end twenty thousand United States Marines had landed.

Five days later two marine divisions began a torturous drive north engaging the Japanese in battle in the hills, cliffs, and caves of the rough central and northern areas of the fifteen-mile-long island. On July 9, 1944, the Fourth Marine Division reached Marpi Point and secured the island.

The local people had been told that the Americans would torture them and commit unspeakable atrocities. They fled the advancing marines, hiding in the hills and caves, and finally, at the island's northern extremity, Suicide Cliff. Marpi Point, near the north end of Saipan, adjoins Suicide Cliff.

The Marines used public address systems to assure the people that they would not be harmed. In spite of their efforts, many thousands leaped over the eight-hundred-foot cliff to the rocks below. A photo taken during the war at Suicide Cliff shows a woman with a baby on her hip standing on the edge, ready to jump. Near her, with arms outstretched, stood a Marine frantically pleading with her. Not understanding English and too frightened to realize his intent, she jumped. The battle involving the securing of Saipan was "the beginning of the end" of the war, according to General Holland M. Smith of the Marine Corps.

The historic problem the FEBC men faced when seeking land sites on Saipan for a local Northern Marianas radio station and land for overseas broadcasts to Asia was complex. Land had been confiscated from private individuals by both occupying forces. The United States had promised to return the land to its owners when the occupation ended.

Unfortunately, land ownership records were destroyed in the holocaust, and there was no legal way to ascertain the rightful owners. The task of working out the rightful ownerships fell to the local government. Forty years had passed, but the local people were not satisfied.

When FEBC arrived on Saipan, some of the people feared that here was another organization that would require more Saipanese land. Emotions erupted. FEBC spent several years searching for land for the local station antenna. Although government negotiations were completed on paper, building was stopped because of the unrest.

Since no land was available for the KSAI antenna, a long wire was stretched between two trees on the property where the studio and transmitter were located. To the amazement of everyone, the signal could be heard very well over Saipan!

Roy Alvarez, who had spent many years as program director for the Manila stations, came with his family to manage the broadcasting of KSAI. In order to gain the acceptance of the local community of Chamorro islanders, he initiated an intensive public relations approach. This involved local news, announcements of public interest and government affairs on a personal level—anything that involved everyday life on the island. Family bereavements were noted. A program of information regarding available work positions was broadcast. It soon became known that anyone with a public announcement or some personal possession to sell could give the announcement to KSAI, and it would be placed on the air. At strategic times during the day, carefully chosen religious segments were inserted between music and the public service announcements. The honest effort proved effective.

When the officials of the government radio station saw that KSAI was serving the community, they said, "You're doing such a good job, it isn't necessary for our station to operate." They took it off the air, and the whole island depended on KSAI for weather reports.

Some who originally had been suspicious of FEBC showed a friendly attitude by stopping by the station. As one person put it, "You're one of us now."

Far East Broadcasting Company decided to raise the power from one thousand to ten thousand watts, enabling the signal to cover the entire Northern Marianas chain more effectively. Excitement ran high with the prospect of reaching more of the isolated people in the vast Pacific area. A ten-thousand-watt transmitter, donated to FEBC by a station in Southern California, was suitable for the Saipan local station.

A long ridge stretched from Capital Hill in the center of the island to the north end of Saipan. Ted Haney, FEBC executive director at the time, saw that it was a good place to build overseas broadcasting stations. The Saipan land commission said that if a suitable site could be found along that ridge, they would assign it to FEBC for the overseas transmitting site.

Norman Blake and Don Bower set off from Capital Hill on an afternoon hike along the elephant grass-covered ridge. When they came to Marpi Cliff they saw potential. The sloping land on a four-hundred-foot cliff above the ocean promised clear shortwave takeoff paths for a full 165-degree sweep from Russia in the north and across China and all

Southeast Asian countries as far south as Indonesia. They had found a perfect international broadcasting site, and the land commission granted the application.

Four hundred feet below Marpi Cliff, the island's main roadway ran from north to south. Before reaching Suicide Cliff, a rocky road turned east. It wound its way to the top of a narrow, sharply ascending ravine, dark with vegetation, lined with caves and rugged rocks. Papaya trees, elephant grass, and tangin-tangin bushes darkened the passage. The road opened onto a broad expanse of land that sloped gently down to the edge of a four-hundred-foot limestone cliff. The view expanded northwest over the limitless sea. This was Marpi Cliff, FEBC's newest overseas transmitting site.

Up that same cave-lined ravine the final battle for Saipan had been fought, and thousands of American and Japanese soldiers died. One reason this choice piece of land had not been purchased was that some of the local people were reluctant to come to this place where they said, "At night we can still hear the moaning of the dead."

Clearing the vine-tangled jumble of elephant grass and tangin-tangin growth was no easy task. More critical was the fact that it had been an ammunition dump during the war. A fire ignited after a horrifying battle, and twenty million dollars worth of ammunition blew up in a tremendous explosion.

However, not all the ammunition exploded. Over eight thousand individual pieces of mortar shells, hand grenades, and other ammunition were removed by the brave FEBC personnel as they cleared the land for construction.

Marpi Cliff was finally ready for the building of the international broadcasting stations to reach billions in Asia with the gospel of Jesus Christ. The passion of those who struggled for Saipan was conveyed by engineer Byrd Brunemeier:

At last! At last! We occupy the land! After five long years of disappointment and debacles, men and machines have arrived to stay on Marpi Cliff. Our twelve acres of "promised land" have been certified by experts in the field as one of the most ideal shortwave broadcast sites ever seen. It not only offers us a perfect saltwater transmission field, but the very height of the cliff itself adds that much "free" height to our antenna towers.

From the first day we went in to hack survey trails through the covering jungle, we could not miss the evidence that our new land was badly stained with the poison of the Pacific War. Rusting artillery shells and hand grenades lay scattered in profusion everywhere, no less deadly after lying dormant for thirty-six years in solitude. Retrieved from flaking sheet metal canisters, sample crumbs of rocket propellant flared with explosive force when put to the match. Everything was still alive indeed.

The local government, hearing of our formidable harvest, was worried enough to send two Marine demolition experts to help us destroy it safely and totally. This operation provided me with a fascinating education in a field I would not care to pursue as a career. The fine art of demolition is an unforgiving profession. It offers no second chance. Time fuses were rigged to trigger the blast. Once the fire was ignited, we all withdrew to a prudent distance to witness our achievement.

The blast, when it came, was an ugly beauty. With muffled thunder, the surly, black cloud leapt skyward, churning and roiling upward and outward in all directions. It rose five hundred feet into the clear Pacific sky before the trade winds broke its upward surge and dispersed its spreading pall downwind. For a full half minute after the blast, I heard hot shrapnel settling down all over the surrounding woods. Two tons of shattered steel precipitated a heavy afternoon shower!

The following day we fired a second shot, and

again our limpid sky was fouled with the belated pollution of war. Fired from the bottom of a deep ravine, this noxious smoke spout rose even higher than the first, sprinkling surrounding hill slopes with a barrage of charred rubble and searing shrapnel.

From Marpi Cliff into all of Asia soon, an Open Door. The tournament of death that once rocked our island has long since ceased. The residue of battle has been gathered up and purged from the land. From here on, we build upward and outward—roads, power lines, buildings and towers, reaching outward to masses who wait for Life through our Open Door. The door will open as faith and prayer combine to make it so.

Byrd was an intrepid builder of towers and transmitters, a clearer of land, an eloquent writer, an unsurpassed photographer, and a fighter of spiritual enemies.

The president of Far East Broadcasting Company, Bob Bowman, and his wife Eleanor were on a two-month deputation trip in Europe and Scandinavia when they received a telephone call from Home Director Evert Carlson. "Byrd Brunemeier was suddenly taken into the presence of the Lord this morning. I don't know the details yet, but will keep you informed."

Byrd had engineered with FEBC for three decades. He was one of the most careful engineers on the staff. At the time he was preparing KSAI's ten-thousand-watt transmitter for the air. Other engineers working outside the door to the transmitter building called to Byrd but got no answer. Stepping inside the door, they found him slumped over the transmitter—dead. He had fallen into ten thousand volts of electricity.

Shortly later, Don Bower, chief engineer of KSAI, also died. A huge, unexpected wave on the southeast side of

Saipan dashed him from a rocky ledge into the sea's deadly undercurrent.

Hundreds of FEBC staff members and their families have paid a high price for service. They work in dangerous places with dangerous equipment. They willingly face loneliness, weariness, and disease.

A monument to their efforts stands high on Marpi Cliff. Tall orange and white towers contrast with the vivid green of the land and the dark blue of the sea. Ever reaching out beyond the horizon, they cover the largest countries in the world, China and Russia, with hundreds of thousands of watts of transmitter power. The Saipan installation marked the completion of Far East Broadcasting Company's third phase of the thrust to place a powerful ring of witnesses around China called "Open Door to China: Phase III."

Thirty-two powerful long- and shortwave stations in five countries transmit the gospel message three hundred program hours per day in 120 languages and dialects using two million watts of aggregate transmitter power to two-thirds of the world's population.

How did it all begin?

2

The Most Unlikely Candidates

Pushing the gas pedal against the floorboards, the proud eighteen-year-old owner of a beat-up 1929 Ford sped along a dirt road that transversed dusty bean fields. His brown hair was slicked back with a wave, and his blue eyes stared straight ahead. The acres of weeds stretching before him would someday shudder beneath the ear-splitting runway traffic of the vast complex known as Los Angeles International Airport. But on that hot Saturday afternoon in the early thirties, the only sounds were the occasional cry of a sea gull and the distant hum of traffic.

The nation struggled at the bottom of its greatest economic depression, but little interested Bob Bowman besides showing off his car's performance. The spinning, sliding tires sent up clouds of dust, bringing laughter and cheers from the friends who traveled with him.

No thoughts drifted into Bob's mind of what or who might lie across the calm Pacific that was a silver streak beyond the sand dunes. Only daydreams about the world's great motor speedways captured his attention. At that point in Bob's life, winning the Indianapolis 500 was his idea of life's greatest achievement. He seemed a most unlikely candidate to fulfill a plan of God.

God often says: "My ways are not your ways," and His divine timetable for Bob began to tick. Bob Bowman's life, destined to center beyond the vast Pacific Ocean, was about to take an astounding turnaround.

Three thousand miles away on the Atlantic coast, another young man in his early twenties dozed uneasily on a New York subway car. The loud clattering rhythm of the rails provided a lullaby. His dreams were colored by bright lights flashing by, sudden hissing stops and starts, and blasts of stale air caused by the onrush of unnamed odors as the doors opened and closed at every stop. End of the line and back, the all-night journey for a nickel offered cheap lodging for an aspiring actor in a temporary "between jobs" financial pinch. This pattern of living was an accepted norm for those in theatrical careers during the unstable years of the thirties in New York City.

No sacrifice seemed too high a price to pay for achievement, and John Broger soon learned both extremes of the success spectrum. He acted in soap operas on commercial radio and entertained in night clubs. His acting abilities and quick sense of humor provided many opportunities to enjoy the bright lights and promises of success and adulation. In time, he lived in a penthouse, drove an Auburn convertible, and wore tailored suits and monogrammed shirts.

Many people would have considered his life exciting and satisfying. Yet success did not fulfill John. It disappointed him. He wanted to make a move away from it all.

The depression year of 1933 presented two young men—one on the Pacific coast, one on the Atlantic—from different backgrounds, of different temperaments, with different goals, and with little probability of ever meeting. Yet God had destined that they would and that their meeting would have an impact on the lives of millions.

Whom does God choose to serve Him? Not just the

gifted, talented, supereducated, mature, proven achievers. Not only the young ones whose personalities and brilliant minds promise these things. Some men of God possess these personal gifts. Yet often He lays His hands upon the most unlikely candidates.

All God needs to fulfill His plan is a willing heart—the human instrument eager to yield and to be used by Him. Then He supplies His wisdom and His gifts. He teaches, and the hard-hitting lessons learned along the plodding ways of obedience provide Christian maturity. God opens the doors of nations before those who are willing to serve Him and causes greater things to happen than could be imagined. It would be the greatest folly to look back at those achievements and harbor any thoughts that men in their wisdom accomplished them.

To point out this truth we need to return to the dirt field near the ocean in Los Angeles to see the young man who could be called "the Most Unlikely Candidate." Over time, Bob Bowman discovered that sports, fast cars, and having fun no longer fulfilled him. He, too, was at the point of a complete change of direction in his life. He remembered the day when he was a nine-year-old boy who went to the altar in a small church and accepted the forgiveness and new life offered by Jesus Christ. This was a memory laid aside for many years.

When Bob startled his family with the announcement, "I'd like to go to Bible school," one member wasn't surprised. Bob's mother had prayed faithfully for her youngest son.

Many years later Bob said, "I really don't know why I said such an unexpected thing. Perhaps it was partly to head off the remonstrations I knew Mom was going to give me and partly for a deep need I felt to change my life."

Regardless, his proclaimed interest in Bible study threw

everyone into action. Bob's mother made a phone call to her pastor, and Bob found himself in the Southern California Bible School in Pasadena before he could change his mind. However, he and the conservative school were not ready for each other, and Bob had to make a painful turnaround in his life.

Great spiritual maturity does not take place instantly. The school took its share of rocking from the new Christian who had not shed all his rebelliousness before he arrived. One who prayed him toward Christian maturity was a classmate from Florida, Burt Evans, who supplied an important link in the chain of events in this unfolding story.

Vine-covered, brown-shingled, sprawling buildings that crested a small hill in Pasadena made up the Southern California Bible School. Originally built as the Annandale Country Club near the turn of the century, its wide verandas, dark wood paneling, stone fireplaces, and gracious dining rooms provided appropriate facilities for Bible study. The purpose of the school's president and founder, Dr. Harold Needham, and the faculty was to instill the highest spiritual goals in the hearts of the students by studying the Word. Also their aim was to provide an opportunity to develop social qualities and to prepare the students to face any occasion that might arise in their future ministries.

The Southern California Bible School, although emphasizing the deeper work of the Holy Spirit, was interdenominational. This fact served Bob well all his life, giving him an unprejudiced view of the spectrum of Christianity. After that he would look beyond denominational divisions. How else could the message of an undivided Savior reach the far parts of the world where people worship innumerable gods?

Behind the speaker's platform in the chapel, a map greeted Bob every morning. The whole world spread before his eyes with its needs calling out. Over it in carved letters, touched with gold, William Carey's words shone: "Attempt Great Things for God—Expect Great Things from God."

One day Bob walked to class with a beloved teacher and will forever remember her brief remark. "Mother Farmer" peered over her eyeglasses and said, "Bob, what you are to Jesus Christ is far more important than anything you will ever do for Him." That challenge became his spiritual lodestar. Bob vowed "to be" for Christ in the inner man, and "to do" for Christ whatever He wanted. Then, with a heart of faith through the power of the Holy Spirit, he expected God to accomplish great things through him. This became the balance on which he weighed all decisions. He knew God could do anything with a life that wouldn't touch the "gold" or the "glory."

In September 1933 his first year at Bible school, Bob met Eleanor Guthrie. She was petite with a gentle sense of humor. Bob said, "She was a pretty, soft-spoken, cultured girl with artistic gifts, and I was a young 'wild-wind' with a lighthearted outlook, one who had lived for athletics and a good time."

While exact opposites in personalities, they shared a desire to serve the Lord Jesus Christ in their daily lives, and they looked to the Holy Spirit for guidance. Neither of them, however, visualized the changes God would fashion in them through the coming years in preparation for their lives together and the ministry already in His Divine planning.

While they studied at Southern California Bible School, talk arose about the miracle of the human voice traveling at the speed of light and how this could be used as a wonderful instrument for spreading the gospel. Even those who were uneasy about radio being "of the devil" began to see its potential for evangelism.

One Saturday, Bob Bowman and Ernie Payne chatted on

the pleasant, wide back veranda of the school. Two men walked up the steep roadway that circled behind the buildings and introduced themselves.

"We're first and second tenors starting a radio ministry, and we need a baritone and a bass singer to complete a male quartet. Do you know any here at the Bible school?"

Bob said, "I sing baritone and Ernie sings bass."

One man replied, "Let's try you out. And by the way, we're looking for an organist. Do you happen to know one on campus?"

Just then Lorin Whitney came out of a building and walked toward them. "There's your organist," replied Bob.

They walked down to one of the school's music rooms and sang together. Thus began the first Haven of Rest quartet and exciting years of ministry for Bob.

The "Haven of Rest" program, with a special ministry to the unsaved, lonely, and heartbroken, began when a man, penniless and ruined by drink, fell to his knees on the floor of a dingy San Diego waterfront hotel with a Gideon Bible before him. Outside in the fog, ships' bells and whistles sounded warning, while Paul Myers asked God for another chance. He received new life that night and was reunited with his praying wife and family.

Before he had begun the inevitable downward slide that ended with his life completely wrecked by alcohol, he had been highly successful in the radio and entertainment world living far from God. Although Paul had no money left, his assets lay in his skill of using the microphone, his compelling radio voice, his unsurpassed talent for reading poetry, and his knowledge of the Word of God, learned from his mother when he was young. His former days in radio gave him contact with commercial radio stations. Now he gave these talents to God to draw individuals like himself back from their wanderings. The harbor sounds that echoed in his ears that night when he returned to God became the theme of the new program. The show began with the sound of a ship's bells and the quartet humming a few bars of the old hymn, "The Haven of Rest."

Then Paul, who was known to his listeners as Bob, said, "Ahoy there, shipmates, eight bells and all's well. This is First Mate Bob and the crew of the Good Ship Grace at anchor in a quiet harbor called Haven of Rest. Come aboard awhile and think about the things that really count."

The quartet sang the beloved hymns, and Paul talked in his easy personal style, "gently pulling in the net." Thousands found Christ.

Because this was one of the first Christian radio programs with an imaginative theme, the listener response was phenomenal. The first program aired in 1934 on KMPC in Beverly Hills, "the Station of the Stars." Then it went on KNX, the large CBS station, where it held a record of the largest number of letters received in a single day by any secular or religious program. The show aired on the NBC Blue Network three times weekly up and down the west coast and across the nation on Sundays. This costly radio time, which would amount to hundreds of thousands of dollars today, was donated free by the network.

During the beginning years the crew had little money. They traveled to and from the "all live" broadcasts in a Model A Ford—three in the front, two in the rumble seat, balancing the vibraharp across their laps.

An enthusiastic response from the listeners resulted. When they toured along the coast, churches and large auditoriums filled to capacity. When they tossed the "net," the altars brimmed over with people from all walks of life seeking the Lord Jesus.

During the first two-and-a-half years of the Haven of Rest program, Bob Bowman continued attending Southern

California Bible School. He and Eleanor graduated in June 1936. The following May they married. Then Bob gave his full time to the ministry of the Haven of Rest. He often took First Mate Bob's place while Paul traveled with a substitute quartet or when Paul's voice, which was subject to laryngitis attacks, failed him. The First Mate affectionately called him "Bobby" and dubbed him "Second Mate Bob." Bob's speaking voice was suited to radio, and day by day he learned from the "master broadcaster" Paul.

The more Bob thought about the ministry, the more he realized the value of radio to reach masses with a message. The crew helped answer thousands of letters from people across America. Some had spiritual needs or questions, and others wrote to tell of receiving Christ while listening to the program. The evidence was clear. God's Word sent over the airwaves could reach the listeners' hearts where they were, whatever the need.

To be on the front lines in the use of radio, to feel the boost of the program's popularity, to be richly rewarded in seeing the number coming to Christ excited Bob. The additional avenues for service were endless.

Bob and Eleanor bought a little home with a "white picket fence and ruffled curtains" and enjoyed happy years with their two young sons, many friends, and ministry opportunities. Besides the "Haven of Rest" programs, Bob accepted invitations to sing and speak in pulpits of many evangelical denominations and organized and directed choirs in churches.

Daily lessons brought a beautiful quality to his voice, and during this time he recorded hundreds of hymns. Paul Myers trained Bob to fill his place on the "Haven of Rest" when he retired. More and more he spoke as well as sang on the programs. Who would want to change a life like that? Yet the Holy Spirit began to whisper.

Sometimes, when Bob sat on the platform at a Haven of Rest church meeting and watched people come to the altar, an alien unrest stirred in his heart. The world map that hung in the chapel of the Southern California Bible School repeatedly appeared in his mind. He pondered its vast expanses of lands untouched by the gospel, some inaccessible to missionaries. *Plenty of non-Christians need to be reached here in America* was the thought with which he tried to dismiss the uneasiness.

The Holy Spirit continued to speak gently but persistently to Bob's heart until this question gelled in his mind. *If radio can bring nonbelievers to Christ in this country, why not use it to reach people in far away places where they have vast populations and little or no witness of Christ?*

Meanwhile in New York City, John Broger searched through books on philosophy and psychology. Existentialism, hot on the scene, temporarily appealed to him, but ultimately he found it unsatisfactory. He turned his back on the New York lifestyle, sold many of his possessions, and returned to his home in Miami.

Several years later Burt Evans, who attended Southern California Bible School with Bob and Eleanor, returned to Florida. Burt was a friend of John's from high school, but they had lost touch. Through God's leading, they met again "by chance" on a Miami beach that summer and renewed their friendship. Burt witnessed to John carefully and easily, not pushing—until one day he asked if they could pray together.

John said, "Sure, why not?"

John later told what happened next. "I started with what little I knew: 'Our Father, who art in heaven. . . .' Then suddenly I experienced an absolutely blinding, dazzling revelation that I knew came from the Lord. I realized for the first time why my life had seemed empty. I wept.

"That was on August 26, 1936. About three weeks later, I boarded a train and headed for the Southern California Bible School."

Because of their friendship with Burt and mutual interest in radio, John and Bob became good friends. John shared his new idea. "I want to develop exciting radio programs to present stories of missionary life from William Carey and other missionary patriarchs to those of today."

"That's a great idea," Bob replied. "I've seen the dramatic and exciting lives of missionaries often presented in a dreary way. Perhaps this happens because many tell their own stories with genuine humility."

"Or they've submerged themselves for so long in another culture far away that it becomes mundane to them. Perhaps they find it hard to translate years of experiences to interest those at home in the few minutes granted to them in pulpits," suggested John. "We can dramatize their stories for them on radio to spark interest and excite people about missions!"

Soon John met his ideal girl in Dorothy Smeltzer, an unusually attractive, talented classmate. The two couples became close friends, attended concerts, laughed, sang, and enjoyed Chinese dinners together. Continually the subject of missions arose. They shared a common wish to serve Christ and a common dream that radio could be used to reach the minds and hearts of many. Somehow China always seemed to surface in their discussions.

At a later date Bob said, "Sometime during those long happy discussions, the vision took shape. The Lord changed our desire to produce missions programs for the stateside radio to the much more challenging and sacrificial vision of building radio stations in the Orient ourselves."

Meanwhile the Holy Spirit challenged, *Don't just tell it—go, and live it!*

Bob continued, "There it was in our hearts—startling us, frightening us with impossibilities, challenging us with the need. We realized the comfortable plans of our lives would be changed. Often, after dinners together, we would pore over a map of faraway, mysterious places. Our eyes always gravitated to China, and we prayed for the Spirit's guidance into our impossible dream."

Then December 7, 1941—Pearl Harbor was bombed, and America went to war. All plans and dreams remained "on hold" for years.

John and Dorothy had married in February of that year. John enrolled in electronics studies and qualified as a radio technician. He entered the navy in 1942 as second class petty officer scheduled for radar. He became an instructor and wrote radar textbooks; then he was assigned to Task Force 38 as warrant officer radio electrician; and ultimately he was promoted to lieutenant and intelligence officer. During the last years of World War II, he saw combat activity with Admiral Halsey's fleet in the Pacific aboard the aircraft carrier *Bon Homme Richard*.

Meanwhile, Bob, a minister and the father of two young children, continued in radio broadcasting in the United States and worked in military service clubs. In his heart the hope of the new dream burned, and he eagerly shared it with any who would hear. One listener was W. J. Roberts, a young pastor in a church where Bob had organized and trained a radio choir.

The war ended September 2, 1945, and part of the Pacific Fleet, including the *Bon Homme Richard,* was due into San Francisco Bay for All Armed Forces Day in November. This was an incredible victory celebration. It was a historic moment for America and an historic moment for the Brogers and the Bowmans.

Eleanor accompanied Dorothy on her trip to San Francisco to meet her husband. John and Dorothy, still considered newlyweds, planned a joyful reunion. Bob was on an evangelistic trip in the Northwest, and the four met in San Francisco.

The victorious Pacific Fleet planned to sail under the Golden Gate Bridge after long years of war. The nation rejoiced, and San Francisco was at gala pitch. Every possible hotel room was reserved for a United States naval officer, and Dorothy reserved a room at the famous Palace Hotel for John and herself. Bob tried in vain to locate a room for himself and Eleanor. As a last resort, he called an old friend who had influential contacts. Soon they found themselves accommodated at the very exclusive Mark Hopkins Hotel on Nob Hill.

Before going to the hotel, John took them to the wharf and escorted them aboard the kamikaze-scarred aircraft carrier. It was obvious that God had spared John's life through dangerous years for a greater purpose.

At dinner John spoke of his recent experiences aboard the warship in the Pacific in a way that left them transfixed. They had prayed for him, and now they heard how the Lord had protected him. When the four went to the Bowmans' reserved room on the sixteenth floor of the Mark Hopkins Hotel, they were astounded to find themselves in the presidential suite.

Huge picture windows looked down on San Francisco Bay where the victorious fleet lay anchored. Every ship's searchlights arced and crisscrossed the sky, reflecting on the waters. The night was ablaze with the lights of the city and the two famous bridges. In the distance the lights of Oakland and Sausalito sparkled across the black water. What a sight it was! World War II was over, and everybody and everything erupted in celebration.

They never could have arranged such an unhampered view themselves, and the four friends reveled in the spectacle. The room was elegantly decorated with a marbleized glass fireplace, luxurious down sofas, and exquisite Chinese lacquered chairs. They gathered around the grand piano and sang while Dorothy played. They talked deep into the night. Little by little the subject of the conversation turned to the future. Kneeling together they laid their hearts before the Lord for His will.

"Would you be willing to leave the Haven of Rest ministry?" John asked.

Bob had thought long and carefully about this for years and now the time for decision had come. "Yes, I'd be willing to leave even though it's a great ministry and I've enjoyed it immensely. We're willing to follow the Lord in this new direction. How do you and Dorothy feel about the future? I know you have tempting career openings before you."

"We want God's will above all else."

Wars don't end every day. Old friends don't meet again every day. Life-changing decisions aren't made every day. Yet, the Holy Spirit called. That spectacular night at the Mark Hopkins Hotel on Nob Hill in San Francisco would always be treasured in their memories. The festive city and light-spangled harbor below provided an unforgettable scene for two couples who had come to a crossroads together. They could never have pictured the roads that lay ahead, but they were willing to attempt great things for God.

December 20, 1945, one month later, having scraped together a thousand dollars out of their personal accounts and having invited Pastor W. J. Roberts to join them as the third party, they incorporated Far East Broadcasting Company.

CHAPTER

3

Through the Door of Commitment

Stepping out on a venture of faith is like being propelled swiftly down an unknown path in the dark. There is confidence and excitement instead of fear. If the way leads suddenly over the edge of a cliff, faith says the foot will find support if God underwrites the venture.

The incorporation papers of Far East Broadcasting Company stated that the organization would be nonprofit, noncommercial, and interdenominational; it would cooperate with all evangelical organizations. However, there was no missionary organization, no board, no foundation, no denomination, and no wealthy underwriter backing the operation. There was no example to follow. No precedent for this sort of endeavor had been attempted in the Orient. The war years had devastated Asia, especially the areas to which Bob and John wanted to go. They owned no transmitters, and they had no staff members. There was nothing in their hands except a vision from God and the faith to follow.

God chose two very different men and brought them together in His mysterious design.

Bob seldom counted the cost.

John always did.

Bob, full of faith that anything could be done, surged toward a challenge with enthusiasm and excitement.

John looked things over calmly and carefully, assessed the cost, and went ahead when the plan was clear.

Bob loved people and people loved him.

John, more reserved in nature, earned the respect of those who got to know him and his thoughtful approach to problems.

This combination of abilities and personalities formed a perfect complement. Each partner possessed qualities the other needed. Each supplied the ministry well with his unique talents.

John planned, Dorothy organized, Bob met the public, and Eleanor helped with publications and took care of the family. Yet each did a bit of every job.

The pulpits of many evangelical denominations welcomed Bob. His long years in the ministry had earned him the credibility and trust necessary to stand before these congregations. He and John effectively communicated the vision to build radio stations in Asia to broadcast the gospel to those who had never heard. Part of the miracle was that pastors invited them to speak of this dream.

Far East Broadcasting Company did not ask God for a master plan or an underwriting of financial support or even a few dollars in advance before taking a step. Yet soon individuals began to support FEBC, realizing that it was a vision given by God.

The next person to join in full-time service to the ministry was Richard Bronson. He and his wife, Marge, had been missionaries in Eastern Europe. Hitler's advances into Danzig had driven them out of Europe, and caring for their severely handicapped child prevented their return. Their missionary hearts responded to FEBC's goals. Dick took charge of home office work. The first Far East Broadcasting headquarters was located in a small Sunday school classroom loaned to them during the week, but needed by the church on weekends. The first mailing address was Box R, Hyde Park Station, Los Angeles, California. Soon they had their own office in a small storefront building. Later they moved to an office building at Third and Ardmore in Los Angeles.

In January of 1946 Far East Broadcasting Company printed the first folder that encapsulated the goal of the newly formed company called "Eyes of the World Toward the Far East." It contained these prophetic words describing the intent of the organization: "A plan to establish a powerful master-transmitter at some central point to cover the complete Far Eastern sphere—subsidiary stations—smaller power stations in densely populated areas. Plan to distribute radio receivers."

In March a ticket was purchased for John's passage on the old *Lane Victory,* the first freighter to leave Los Angeles Harbor for Asia after World War II. John had seen more of the Pacific waters during the war years than he cared to recall. His decision to face them again soon after the war's end was founded on the conviction that he was fulfilling the will of God. The crossing was not easy. He wrote that these were the worst days he had ever spent at sea, and he had endured plenty. Torrential storms prevented anyone from standing up or walking around the freighter.

A month later he arrived at the mouth of the Yangtze River and traveled to Shanghai. Here John stayed at China Inland Mission headquarters and conferred and prayed with James Hudson Taylor II, son of the great missionary to China.

John proceeded with the business of obtaining a franchise for broadcasting stations from the Chinese government. As he traveled from one office to another, he became oppressed by the great suffering he saw, and he renewed his dedication to bring China the message of hope.

The Chinese Nationalist government, far from well organized, feared the oncoming Communist movement. They were uneasy about dispensing broadcasting power. John found that no one would say "yes" and no one would say "no." They did suggest that an application for five-hundred-watt stations might be considered, but weak transmissions would have been useless for trying to reach China's millions.

Back in Los Angeles, Bob gave his farewell address on the "Haven of Rest" broadcast on May 1. It was difficult for him, for he had loved his twelve years of ministry.

First Mate Bob donated a thousand dollars toward the work and offered to put the FEBC folder through the Haven of Rest mailing list. He said that the names of those who answered could be placed on the new organization's mailing list. Six hundred people responded.

Bob started an extensive itinerary through the churches wherever there was an open door. The vision began to spread.

Meanwhile, John moved on to Nanking, Hangchow, and Macao. Still all doors were closed. After many weeks he returned to Shanghai and submitted an application to the government for a franchise to build and operate six five-hundred-watt stations to be located in heavily populated areas. Perhaps these applications are still pending today.

While he waited, he realized that a recording studio was of great importance to get Chinese programming underway. The people of the China Inland Mission, with their deep concern for reaching China's millions, warmly opened to the vision of what radio could do. They graciously allowed the studio to be set up in their headquarters, and transcribing equipment was prepared in Los Angeles to ship to Shanghai. This meant cutting discs and records, a long involved process. An FEBC Chinese board of directors was organized, made up of five outstanding Chinese laypeople and clergy who grasped the vision of reaching China by radio.

The franchise to build a powerful broadcasting station in China was not forthcoming. Still John did not feel defeated when he left for the Philippines. He felt led. Yet only God knew that China's bamboo curtain was swinging closed, and any effort FEBC put forth in China would be lost three years later.

John arrived in the Philippines two days after the war-torn country received its independence on July 4, 1946, and became a new republic. The city of Manila lay in shambles; the debris of World War II was heaped everywhere, littering the streets. Said to be the most "shot up" city of the war, it had been virtually leveled.

Japanese troops had landed on Luzon on December 10, 1941, three days after they bombed Pearl Harbor. General MacArthur concentrated his outnumbered Filipino and American troops on Bataan peninsula and Corregidor island in Manila Bay. In spite of their heroic resistance, they surrendered in May of 1942. MacArthur left the Philippines with his famous promise, "I shall return," but it was February, 1945, before the Philippines was recaptured.

The Filipinos had suffered greatly at the hands of the Japanese. The fiendish water cells for bloodless executions, originally constructed by the Spanish, were reactivated at Fort Santiago. There the helpless victims drowned at high tide. Ten thousand Filipino and American soldiers died of starvation or mistreatment on the seventy-mile Bataan death march through the dense jungle to concentration camps.

John realized that in the midst of the destruction left by World War II, getting the Philippine government into operation was a gigantic problem. Government offices were housed in bombed-out buildings on the verge of collapse. In the final bombings of the city, many government records had been destroyed, including land titles.

In spite of overwhelming difficulties, Christian work was already in progress in Manila. American GI Christians were making great efforts to help. At a Sunday service John met a man who asked, "What are you doing here, now that the war is over?"

"I'm trying to get in contact with the proper government officials to build some Christian radio stations in the Philippines," John replied.

"Maybe I can help you."

The man's name was Leon O. Ty. He was an attorney and one of the most respected journalists in the Philippines. Later Mr. Ty took John to the office of the secretary of justice, who was responsible for radio control in the new governmental structure.

"We are a noncommercial organization . . ." John explained.

"What do you mean, 'noncommercial'? You mean there will be no commercial broadcasting on your stations?"

"Yes, sir," John said. "That's right."

The secretary shook his head, puzzled. "How in the world will you live then?"

John tried to explain what Hebrews 11:1 meant. "Now faith is the substance of things hoped for, the evidence of things not seen."

The secretary of justice replied, "Well, I don't know what kind of faith that is, but if you think you can live on it, we might give you an opportunity to do so."

John wrote home, "Living quarters are almost impossible to find in Manila, and land is very expensive."

When the government granted the permit to FEBC, the officials wanted to know the exact future location of the transmitters and studios. John requested a couple of days before answering.

Two Christian businessmen in Manila had twelve and one-half acres for sale valued at approximately fifty thousand dollars. After consulting with the two owners of the property and setting before them the aims of FEBC, the entire plot was offered for twenty thousand dollars. John Broger used his last dollars to secure an option on the land. Having no money, John "hitched" a ride back home on a United States Air Force plane.

Back in the United States, Far East Broadcasting Company launched a week of prayer to raise the needed funds. On Thanksgiving Day, FEBC still found itself short by four thousand dollars. The next day more letters were received in the postal box than ever before. The donations totaled $6,062. The property was purchased.

A Chicago man, whom none of them had met, wrote that the Holy Spirit had spoken to him, telling him to "send a check for five thousand dollars to those young men out in California who have a vision for building a missionary radio station in the Orient." He sent it.

When filing the final documents for the franchise, FEBC had requested permission for two ten-thousand-watt transmitting stations. There were not many broadcasting stations in the international bands in those days. At the time that would have been sufficient power to send a good signal all over Asia. Yet God knew that in the coming years many nations around the world would begin to build international radio stations. Before returning the approved document, *someone* in the radio control office had crossed out the phrase "ten thousand watts of power." In pencil, written over it were the words "Unlimited Power!" Since then, the Philippine government has granted FEBC more and more power—50,000, 100,000, even 250,000 watts of power.

Two Steps at a Time

A shiny yellow Jeep with bulldozing blade raised high bounced along the bomb-gutted streets of Manila. It plowed a path through a melange of jeepneys crammed with people, chickens, and an occasional pig. The vehicle swerved to miss battered trucks overloaded with heavy equipment and miniature horses that drew two-wheeled calesas.

It was January 1947, and former chaplain Arvid Viedmark had returned to the war-damaged Philippines to clear the Far East Broadcasting Company land and start building. He and his family had arrived at Manila Bay a few hours before on an old freighter. They disembarked onto the pier amid smells of crated fish blended with odors of tar, oil, bilge water, copra, and tobacco.

After claiming his Jeep and arranging for the equipment to follow, Arvid tried to maneuver his new vehicle toward the National Highway. Away from the noise of the city, he turned off the highway onto an exceedingly bumpy roadway called Pugad Baboy (Pig's Nest Road). The narrow lane was bordered on both sides by open sewers. With his family he passed nipa huts where curious Filipinos leaned out windows to see the blond American children. He drove by high walls topped with jagged glass set in concrete that enclosed larger Filipino homes.

When they turned onto the FEBC property, Arvid stopped the Jeep and stared at an uncontrolled jungle, tightly choked with vines and weeds. Giant termite hills encased the trees that had once been an orderly orchard. Huge rats and lizards scuttled through the undergrowth, enjoying the rotting fruit.

An old Filipino house stood by the gateway under a large santol tree. Built of wood with a tin roof, it was set about six feet above the ground on wooden poles. It had Philippine mahogany floors, capiz (shell) sliding windows, and a primitive charcoal cooking grate.

Arvid, Lois, and their small children moved in and made friends with the Filipino neighbors. Arvid dug a well that he shared with the villagers. Gladys and Kenneth Short, missionaries posted in Borneo, joined the Viedmarks.

Because the new Philippine Republic was rebuilding itself from the ashes and rubble of war, building materials were in short supply. Cement was high on the government reconstruction priority list, but not a single day was lost in building for lack of it. Miraculously, through negotiations FEBC was placed in the important buildings category in Manila. Filipino workmen helped Arvid pour cement for the foundations and floors of the studio and transmitter building. Then with crude tools they began on the structural parts of the buildings.

Meanwhile, Bob and John were in the United States trying to raise the thousands of dollars needed. They produced a radio program known as "The Call of the Orient" on which they sang duets and solos, dramatized the lives of missionaries, and spoke of the vision.

Ralph Carmichael organized his first orchestra, and the program was produced on the Moody Institute of Science sound stage under the direction of Dick Ross. There were no tapes in those days, just large acetate-covered metal discs on which fifteen-minute programs could be recorded. A mistake meant redoing the entire program. Christian and secular radio stations aired these programs without charge.

Other people joined the FEBC staff. They held services, printed literature, purchased electronic materials, and recruited additional staff. FEBC's first engineers, Richard Rowland and Richard Handlos, completed the first small transmitter in an old chicken coop belonging to Bob's parents.

In the fall of 1947 an urgent cablegram came from Arvid: "The Philippine Government demands that FEBC be on the air by April 4, 1948!"

Manila was seven thousand miles away, and passage for the sixteen new staff members and fifty-two tons of equipment cost $10,180. There was nothing in FEBC's checking account.

Yet God placed the need on the hearts of His people, and the funds arrived by sailing time. Headed by John, the staff members and their families sailed out of San Francisco on February 23, just two months before the impossible deadline. Dorothy Broger and a second group of missionaries followed on a ship laden with broadcasting equipment. How was it humanly possible to uncrate, set up, and test the transmitter; complete the studio; and build an antenna system by the time the government demanded that they start the broadcasts?

From the moment of disembarking in Manila two and a half weeks later, John Broger and the small staff of carpenters and engineers expended their full energies to see the "impossible task" completed. They were joined by many Filipinos who worked with them. But the deadline could not be met. Building materials cost too much to buy enough to finish the structures without additional funds. Then a devastating typhoon hit Manila and ravaged the compound. It was followed by three weeks of unrelenting rains blown horizontally at times by the fury of the wind. Because the houses only had siding and no window panes, beds, clothing, books, and equipment were soaked. The compound oozed with mud.

FEBC asked for and obtained a seven-week extension of time. John wrote to the home office: "We gather for prayer in the morning, and the Lord continually reminds us that we are more than conquerors in Christ Jesus. We have confidence in Him. Everyone is in good health. The buildings are going up. The electronic equipment is being installed, and we thrill with anticipation of on-the-air day."

The name Christian Radio City Manila was tagged onto the twelve and a half acres that was shaping up to clipped green lawns and trimmed fruit trees. The title stuck. It has been CRCM ever since. On June 4, 1948, a wind, teasing with raindrops that never fell, whipped the colorful Philippine flag against the gray sky. It was raised in front of the still unpainted transmitter building while strains of the Philippine national anthem caused proud backs to straighten and heads to lift. The white Christian flag, with its red cross standing out in a field of blue, was raised to fly beside the Philippine flag. The Far East Broadcasting Company's first station, DZAS, went on the air at 6:00 P.M. The hymn "All Hail the Power of Jesus' Name" radiated its majestic message into the Asian airwaves. The overworked group of missionaries and Filipinos gathered briefly and then went back to work.

The listening audience across the Philippines could not see this scene, but the signal they received brought a message of hope and life. Nor could they see antenna lead-in wires hung temporarily across poles for support. Wires from the power plant were strung across makeshift poles to the rear of the transmitter where water was sometimes ankle deep. Pioneering radio was not safe, smooth, or elegant. Yet eventually the equipment was installed properly, and the buildings were completed.

The Bowman family came in 1949 to exchange places with the Brogers. As codirectors, the two families planned to trade places every year and a half or two years. One family would be stationed on the field to direct and the other on the home front to raise money that was needed in growing amounts.

With DZAS on the AM mediumwave serving Manila and the surrounding area, FEBC reached out to the outer islands. In 1949 shortwave station, DZH6, went on the forty-nine-meter band to reach beyond the Philippines into China. The vision expanded. The staff focused their eyes beyond the horizon.

In 1951 John held a seminar at CRCM attended by delegates from Burma, Hong Kong, Vietnam, Indonesia, Japan, Malaysia, Russia, Thailand, and the Philippines. He addressed the language supply problem and reviewed the challenges of the work. The FEBC staff realized the need to develop language programs using national voices.

During those first years, living on the compound was a challenge to the new arrivals and to many who joined them at CRCM. They learned to live in unfinished houses and adjust to the extremes of tropical climate. The homes were not air-conditioned, and heat rashes became common. As deeper wells were drilled, sometimes the water supply was temporarily cut off.

The FEBC families learned to live with hordes of ants, giant cockroaches, and the ubiquitous tiny lizards darting about on every wall and screen. They were not alarmed by the occasional rat and shrew, but they took special note of the few cobras that raised their heads in challenge when their hiding places were discovered.

The children played happily in the compound. Their mothers taught them with correspondence courses until one missionary woman became their teacher.

Most doctors had left the Philippines to serve in the war, and few had returned. With the help of a missionary nurse from the Bible Institute next door, FEBC staff learned simple ways to deal with sudden illnesses.

Veteran missionaries to the Philippines, who had been interned by the Japanese during the war, had since been sent back to the United States where they were recovering. In the early years there was no one to guide the new radio missionaries in learning the culture. They had to learn Filipino ways from their Filipino coworkers, and the Filipinos learned the puzzling ways of Americans from the Americans. Fortunately, Christian love covered a multitude of errors.

Along with building and engineering, every adult on the compound had a special responsibility for broadcasting: writing programs, announcing, typing, answering listener mail, and writing publications for home. Some preached at local churches on Sunday. Regular prayer meetings and Bible studies were conducted for the new Filipino staff members.

When the tired staff knelt on the cement floors to pray, joy filled their hearts. They knew why they were there and felt gratitude to God for allowing them to be on the front lines to see and hear of those being won for Christ by the broadcasting of His Word. These lines were written on the compound in the early years:

"When Morning Gilds the Sky . . ." Who at Christian Radio City Manila, seeing dawn's forerunning delicate streamers touch buildings and antenna towers with pale gold and then with splendid triumph sweep the arc

of the east with flame, has not said with the songwriter:
"My Heart rejoicing cries, Let Jesus Christ be praised!"

There is an unseen network surrounding the small nucleus of buildings we call the Christian Radio City Manila. The network fans out like a gigantic web with lines extending to embrace half of the earth's circumference. Invisible chains of sound waves are strong and swift linking the stations with listeners in far away places. The strands of sound go out in every direction pushing aside barriers and boundaries and curtains dropped by the enemies of God. Sound waves link us to many lands. A missionary, ill and lonely in a faraway place, is strengthened by the Word of God. A man in Japan or in Malaysia bends over a radio and hears the vital message of Christ for the first time.

Because hundreds of thousands of invisible sound lines bind us tonight to those in many lands, it is our desire that every listener will be drawn to the Focal Point, not a station or a transmitter, but to the Lord Jesus Christ, Himself. That is our prayer at Christian Radio City Manila. Thank you, Lord, for letting us be a part of it.

Gradually the original ideal of FEBC was realized when the national broadcasters assumed more of the leadership. Western missionaries remained as helpers and advisors, but Filipinos such as Fred Magbanua, Bert Dizon, and Efren Pallorina took over administrative roles. Proceso Marcelo began as a guard at CRCM when he was a rebellious teenager. He became a Christian, went to Bible college, and has served ever since with FEBC broadcasting and ministering. Today he is the foremost Christian radio evangelist to his people.

During these beginning years, a group of Communist-led rebels known as the HUKS attempted to seize the government in Manila. They roamed through central Luzon, terrorizing the defenseless outlying villages in the daytime and controlling the outskirts of Manila at night. Sometimes they stepped out of the darkness to stop FEBC cars on the road to CRCM, searching for guns. The Filipino and missionary staff ignored their personal safety and continued to arrive on schedule at the studios, keeping a faithful commitment to reach their kinspeople.

Soon it became evident that CRCM needed a large antenna tower. All they had was a temporary antenna strung between two telephone poles. The engineers urged Bob to find a new tower, but the biggest deterrent was lack of funds.

One day an executive with a large wireless company called CRCM on the phone. "I hear you're looking for an antenna. I know where you can get one."

"Where?"

"Right here in Manila. We have one that we're not going to need. It's war surplus and still in the crates. Also, it's three hundred feet high, self-supported by four legs sixty feet apart at the base, and weighs eighty thousand pounds. Originally the antenna cost about twenty-five thousand dollars. Make a bid."

Bob knew the checking account held only three hundred dollars. He offered that.

The business man sounded surprised. "Well, I'll submit the 'bid' to the home office."

For some reason his San Francisco office accepted it! Within a few days heavy trucks rolled in from the highway with forty tons of steel, pre-cut and formed, for a massive tower that would reach three hundred feet into the sky. An electronic hat would eventually add eight feet to the height.

Radio engineer Byrd Brunemeier arrived with his wife Angie at Christian Radio City Manila shortly before the tower was delivered. With FEBC Engineer Don Geary, he began the job of building the tower. An unexpected problem arose when they discovered the cost of the cement for the four concrete footings. They would have to delay the construction until two thousand dollars could be raised.

One day Chua Kian Tiong, a Chinese broadcaster, walked by the piles of steel. Mrs. Chua led the Chinese Evangelistic Band who had faithfully arrived at the studios every Sunday night during the terror of the HUK raids when some broadcasters from the city were afraid to brave the dangers.

"Why isn't the tower going up?" Mrs. Chua asked Bob, who stood where the tower footings were to be poured. Her English was limited and his Chinese was nonexistent, but they understood each other perfectly.

"One reason," he replied. "We need two thousand dollars for the cement foundations."

She shook her head and murmured, "Too bad, too bad." The next week when Mrs. Chua came to broadcast her program, she stopped by Bob's office and laid a white envelope in front of him. He opened it and found two thousand dollars. She had challenged her Chinese Christian friends to give and thus removed the roadblock. Week after week the work went on. Every piece of heavy steel angle iron had to be lifted by the winch and fitted in place. Men working on the tower secured themselves by their safety belts, but at times they had to depend on their hands as they jockeyed around for another position. The tower continued to go skyward until it was finished the second week in June. Then Don and Byrd climbed down from the top and shook hands at the bottom of the eighty-thousand-pound tower. Meanwhile, other FEBC engineers worked feverishly to increase the power of the transmitters.

Letters began to arrive. Not only did they encourage the staff, but they served as the impetus toward completing new transmitters. People tuned in "by accident" and discovered the new broadcasting station. One letter read:

Dear Friends:

I've always listened to dance music on my radio, but last night I happened to turn the dial to your station and heard my own language on the air! I live a long way from Manila, and this was the first time I heard DZAS.

I am sorry my language is only on twice a week. We do not have any missionaries here. I never met any Christians, but the thing you are talking about thrills my heart. I became convicted by the heaviness of sin in my heart. Last night, when I heard of the Lord Jesus Christ, I wanted Him to help me. Now I feel so happy. Please tell me what has happened to me.

Sincerely,
H. Garcia

"Happened to tune in" was a phrase that became common over the years. Another man wrote:

My whole family has been listening to your broadcast for a year now, and at last we believed that Jesus Christ is the Son of God, the true God, and that your religion is correct. We have all accepted Him as our personal Savior.

Although these letters were encouraging, when a technicality took DZAS, the local station, off the air for a short time, the staff seemed to let down in their efforts. The shortwave stations were still on, but the broadcasters seemed focused only on Manila.

As the FEBC staff met for prayer one morning, Bob read John 10:16. "And other sheep I have which are not of this fold; them also I must bring."

This short verse struck to the heart. FEBC dared not confine its efforts only to getting the gospel to the Philippines and other nearby countries. To the north lay Japan. To the south lay Indonesia. To the west lay the lands of Southeast Asia: Vietnam, Laos, Cambodia, Malaysia, Thailand, and Burma. And beyond the Himalayas lay India. Millions spoke a diversity of languages—so many without the gospel.

To the northwest in the massive land of China, missionaries were fleeing from Communist-controlled areas. Chinese Christians began to understand the suffering that lay before them. It became increasingly apparent why God had placed Far East Broadcasting Company in this place at this time.

FEBC engineers determined to press the construction of additional transmitters through to completion as soon as possible. The program staff increased their efforts to produce programs in the languages of other countries. They received cooperation from missionaries and nationals of many evangelical denominations and independent missions.

Then DZAS went back on the air, but now the focus was not just Manila. Their eyes looked beyond the horizon to distant parts of the world.

In the days before Japan built cheap transistors, many people in remote areas could not afford radios. The only way to reach these individuals was to design and construct receivers and place them in villages where radios were not in plentiful supply. A workshop was set up in one CRCM building where assembly-line methods of construction speeded the output.

Far East Broadcasting Company decided that the radios should be used to receive the gospel programming only, so the radios were pre-tuned to FEBC stations. Since the batteries were expensive and had a limited life, FEBC did not want the radios used to pick up any Communist propaganda. Someone called them "portable missionaries," and they have been known as PMs ever since. They are described as follows:

- Preaches the Word of Life many hours daily without tiring
- Speaks many languages or dialects
- Gives the best in gospel music
- Needs no allowance
- Eats no rice
- Will not contract tropical disease
- May be carried to regions inaccessible or hostile to outsiders

Isabelo Montejo, director of the portable missionary department, was the modern-day apostle Paul who distributed and followed up hundreds of these listening outposts throughout the Philippines.

One primitive tribe of seminomadic people on the island of Mindoro had little or no contact with the gospel of Christ. Missionaries had tried to contact the tribe, but the natives always faded away to the inner recesses of the jungle. Missionaries hesitated to make their homes on Mindoro because of the high incidence of malaria.

Two FEBC staff members tried for three weeks to contact the seminomads but failed. As they left, they placed a PM in a nipa hut on the Mindoro shoreline. Word spread across the mountains that there was a "box that could talk" at the seashore. Some Mangyans carefully made their way down to see this strange phenomenon. That visit opened the way to placing PMs among the primitive Mangyan tribes.

Reverend Max Atienza joined Far East Broadcasting Company and became the first Filipino administrative director in Manila. His "Bukas Na Aklat" program, a Bible study in the Tagalog language, drew a wide listening audience. One day Max received an invitation from members of the Mangyan tribe on Mindoro who had been listening to his programs. Max attended a meeting held in his honor. The mayor,

Balik Luna, introduced him to the others. Balik was a handsome man who wore a Western white shirt and a loincloth. He was short in stature as are all the Mangyan people.

The meeting was held in the rain forest under the shade of heavy tropical foliage. These primitive people had never participated in an actual church service, but the PMs gave them the desire to worship together. The "box that talked" had never explained church ritual, so they adopted the only procedure they knew.

When Balik opened the worship service, he stood in their midst and said, "This is Far East Broadcasting Company, Manila." Then he introduced Max, and the people were excited to meet the voice on their radios. When the service was over, the following benediction was pronounced: "Tune in again tomorrow night at this same time."

Later, workers of the Overseas Missionary Fellowship took up residence on Mindoro and began work among these Mangyan people. Today the Mangyans have their own station, which is a cooperation between the Mangyan Tribal Council, the Overseas Missionary Fellowship, and Far East Broadcasting Company. They have around one hundred organized churches among the Mangyans with over eight thousand born-again believers. They send their own missionaries to reach other tribal areas. The PMs are used as preaching evangelists wherever they go.

It seemed that the ministry of FEBC would go forward as planned initially with the Bowmans and Brogers exchanging places in the United States and overseas, until something totally unforeseen happened. The Korean conflict began.

In 1954 John was called to Washington, D.C., for a conference with United States military authorities. Although FEBC has never been politically affiliated in any way, God gave John an insight on the advance of Communism in Asia, which he saw as more than political. A paper he wrote, "Militant Liberty," had come to the attention of government officials, so John was called to the capitol for a forty-five day conference. In time he decided to serve his Lord by dedicating a lifetime of service to his country. Eventually he occupied the post of director of armed forces information and education in the Pentagon.

This decision led to John's resignation from FEBC. He left an admirable Christian testimony when he retired with many honors from his position with the government twenty-three years later. For all the years, though separated in distance and led in separate avenues of service, the Bowmans and the Brogers remained close personal friends.

As time went by, the international airways became more congested. Some world powers, intent on winning the nations with their ideologies, ignored the international laws governing control of frequencies. The assistant chief of the radio control board returned to Manila from the International Conference on Radio Regulation in Geneva. He announced that the Communists refused to abide by the international control of frequencies above six Megahertz.

As a result, FEBC needed to increase the power of its stations with larger transmitters. They had bid successfully on two war surplus "electronic giants" in San Francisco. In 1960 one was sent to the island of Okinawa, a part of the Ryukyuan chain of islands that trail off the southernmost tip of Japan, to be placed on the AM mediumwave broadcasting band to reach China. Okinawa was wrested from the Japanese in the last bloody battle of World War II. In human life, it was the most costly engagement in the Pacific. Soon another FEBC project was under way on that war-torn island.

The other transmitter was shipped to the Philippines, where engineers began the search for suitable land for a new overseas transmitter site. The location had to be far enough away from Manila to satisfy the Radio Control Board but easily accessible to CRCM.

Isabelo Montejo negotiated with owners of rice-paddy land a few kilometers north of CRCM in Bocaue. Lying within tidal rivers and salt marshes, the transmission site was an ideal location. Soon construction on the four-thousand-square-foot transmitter building began, headed by engineer Frank Matias.

FEBC expanded rapidly, and so did the costs. Although prayerful contributors gave generously, lack of funds stopped the expansion projects temporarily on Okinawa and in the Philippines. They needed twenty thousand dollars more than the current operating expenses.

One morning, members of the home-office staff were on their knees praying for that amount. The phone rang. It was Western Union with a telegram: "Within a few days you will receive $20,000." It was signed with a Chinese name, Tsai Lee.

Only later did Bob learn that the funds had been designated for FEBC by Tsai Lee's Christian father, who awaited trial by a Chinese Communist court in Shanghai. Tsai Lee's parents had often listened to the Manila stations in their home in Shanghai. The funding need for the projects, which would give more powerful voices to the China mainland, was unknown to the Lee family. Yet God had spoken to them to send the last of their money they had transferred to a Chicago bank prior to the Communist takeover in China. Through a coded message just before his death, Mr. Lee had communicated his desire to his son, Tsai, in the United States.

The Free World conceded the loss of China, and the Christian world was forced to bow to the formidable barriers to the gospel that arose around China's 452 million people.

Yet FEBC remained faithful to its calling. From 1949 on FEBC steadily increased the power of the signals to China. Then toward the end of the decade another part of God's plan to intersect the barriers around the ancient land began to unfold.

FEBC searched for another land from which to encircle China with God's love. The quest led to the small island of Okinawa.

FEBC built three stations on Okinawa. Arthur Austin designed the transmitter buildings. KSDX broadcast to the Ryukyuans, and KSAB aired for the United States servicemen stationed on the island. On May 1, 1961, at Okuma on the northernmost point of the island, hundred-thousand-watt station KSBU, called "A Mighty Voice to China," began broadcasting on the AM mediumwave band. Listeners in China could pick up this signal on their regular radios.

A few letters began to arrive from China. One read:

> After 1949 the church changed to a school. Then I was discouraged. For fourteen years I have been cut off from communication with a church. I listen to the gospel broadcast. Thank the Lord who gives me a chance to return to the bosom of Jesus, to be close to Him. May God bless you. Your brother in the Lord.

The work progressed. By 1961 Far East Broadcasting Company had expanded to fifteen stations: five AM mediumwave, one FM, and nine shortwave stations penetrating Asia and the Soviet Union. Three operated from Okinawa and eleven from the Philippines. Unexpectedly and under astounding circumstances, FEBC obtained international station KGEI in San Francisco and began broadcasting to all of Latin America.

CHAPTER

5

Hidden Ambassador Beside the Golden Gate

Ricardo glanced at his comrades as they lay half hidden in the Peruvian jungle grass, sound asleep. Plugging the earphone into his radio, he slowly moved the tuner across the dial. It stopped at the spot where Radio Havana's powerful voice spewed out hatred toward its enemies. Ricardo felt a wave of nausea caused by his inner conflicts. His young mind churned with animosity against the rich landlords of his native Peru, who had cheated his parents.

On this hot night, Ricardo was far from home. Injustice had driven him and his comrades into the jungles to fight. Turmoil caused his sleeplessness, a hatred that seethed inside him.

Continuing to move the dial across his radio, Ricardo paused for a moment when a voice identified itself as *"La Voz de la Amistad,"* which means "the Voice of Friendship": "But I say to you, love your enemies, bless those who curse you, do good to those who hate you, and pray for those who spitefully use you and persecute you, that you may be sons of your Father in heaven" (Matt. 5:44–45a).

The young Communist listened intently. He knew he hated his enemies, and suddenly his pent-up feelings burst. Ricardo later wrote in his first letter to FEBC:

I began to weep like a baby. All the hatred in my heart vanished.

Sirs, can you tell me what has happened to me? Oh, if only I could love all people in the world in this way!

Ricardo was afraid to tell his comrades what happened that night. A few days later, after saying good-bye to his guerilla friends, he left to visit his sister's home. How could he explain what happened in the jungle? He thought the best way would be to let her hear the Voice of Friendship. That night they listened together. Again, the announcer spoke the words of Jesus regarding the transformation of a human life through the miracle of being "born again."

"That's it," he said. "That's the reason I can love my enemies when once I was filled with hatred." The new believer possessed a burning desire to share his newfound love with his comrades in the jungle. The answer to their frustration was not in fighting, but in loving. Ricardo returned to the jungle to find his friends and tell them.

Because guerilla fighters generally move from one place to another, it was not easy to find traces of his comrades. He searched for weeks before learning the truth that all of his friends had either been captured or killed in their clandestine warfare. A deep sorrow filled Ricardo's heart because the chance to tell his comrades the good news was gone. Yet he wondered, "Why have I, among all my friends, been allowed to hear this great message of Jesus Christ?"

What should he do? He contemplated the choices. He could return to the city and live at peace with himself and his family, or he could stay in the mountains and help the people there who were as much in need of the message of Jesus Christ as he had been.

Looking to his newfound friend, Jesus, he prayed for

direction. The answer was clear. He would still fight for the people and their needs, but now he would be "a guerilla for Jesus."

As months passed, Ricardo sent many letters to the FEBC station in San Francisco. In several letters he asked for copies of Bible correspondence course materials offered over the air, five copies at a time. Then he asked for ten.

A broadcaster asked what Ricardo was doing with all the literature. Ricardo answered that he had now led forty people in the jungle to Jesus Christ. He was discipling them the best he could with the help of the correspondence courses. He asked for a plot of land from the government, and the new believers built a church. This young former Communist guerilla wrote:

> I am now going out to find a Bible seminary that I can attend to learn more of the gospel so that I can be a better guerilla for Jesus!
>> Your Son in the Faith,
>> Ricardo

Many like Ricardo in every country of Latin America and Cuba have also found faith in Christ. The transforming power of the gospel is the same though their stories vary in detail.

Why have they been able to hear? Because KGEI, veteran missionary station HCJB, and other missionary broadcasting stations send powerful signals their way.

KGEI, *La Voz de la Amistad* (Voice of Friendship), is located on the shoreline of San Francisco Bay, about twenty miles south of the city.

In 1960 FEBC was informed that the powerful international station was on the market. They knew KGEI offered great opportunity for international broadcasting. They were reluctant to pursue the matter since at that time the Philippine projects were expanding and the station building on Okinawa was in full swing. Language centers were opening in several countries, and funds had to be gathered in increasing amounts. FEBC had no surplus money on hand.

Nevertheless, since they were urged to do so, Bob and other staff members went to look at KGEI. They turned east off the Bayshore Highway and drove for two miles on a bumpy dirt road between drying salt beds and brackish tideland waters to the edge of the bay.

At the end of the road stood a weather-grayed two-story structure as impregnable as a World War II pillbox. Wild ducks gathered and sea gulls wheeled over the marshland. Towers rose at the edge of the bay. Winds whipped through the huge, pointed structures and a string of smaller ones. They looked like electronic clotheslines stretching toward the tideland mist.

During World War II KGEI was used by the War Department to broadcast information behind enemy lines across the vast Pacific War theatre. From these towers, the ravaged Filipino fighting troops heard General MacArthur's famous words, "I shall return."

After the war ended, the station owners found commercial international broadcasting unprofitable. KGEI was for sale for a mere $101 thousand! Rumors circulated of bidders with cash in their hands eagerly waiting, but for some reason the owners considered doing business with FEBC. They looked into FEBC's Dun and Bradstreet rating and found it on the A1 page. This impressed the owners.

The owners said that if FEBC would make a down payment of twenty-seven thousand dollars, the rest could be paid over a five-year period. After looking at the station, Bob knew KGEI was a treasure because of its franchise for international broadcasting. Yet he realized that a foolish move could throw the already delicate financial structure of FEBC off balance and endanger the burgeoning overseas projects.

FEBC was given just twenty-four hours to decide if KGEI was a God-given opportunity or a temptation. As Bob turned the car around to drive the four hundred miles back to Los Angeles, he decided to put out a fleece as Gideon did. The others in the car agreed, "If God sends an extra twenty-seven thousand dollars in the next twenty-four hours, we will know it means we should grasp the opportunity." No single contribution of that size had ever been donated to FEBC.

When Bob and the others arrived back at the headquarters they learned that FEBC had just received a legacy from a will of a man no one could remember meeting. The elderly man had sent in contributions of five dollars a month for some time before his death. Now he had bequeathed Far East Broadcasting Company a hundred thousand dollars in his will, and an advance of twenty-seven thousand was immediately available from the legacy. God had answered.

KGEI, named by a newspaper man as the "Hidden Ambassador Beside the Golden Gate", is a multibanded station that broadcasts over five time zones to Latin America and over the North Pole to all eleven time zones of the Soviet Union. This radio station, with 50,000-watt and 250,000-watt transmitters, is one of the most powerful privately owned stations that stands within the continental United States.

FEBC began its Latin American broadcasts in 1960. The schedule was six and a half hours a day, spread over the five time zones of Mexico and Central and South America. Today that schedule has expanded to seventeen hours, making it possible for Latins to hear KGEI both in the morning when they arise and in the evening when they retire.

The uniqueness of KGEI's Latin American service focuses on the theme, *"La Voz de la Amistad."* The objective is to build on the idea of friendship among the people and the nations of what is generally referred to as "El Continente" (Latin American Nations). The program schedule built around this theme includes the popular *"Cadena de Amistad"* (Chain of Friendship or Pen-pal Club), a schedule-long presentation of the music of Latin America from KGEI's huge collection, teaching English to Spanish speakers (complete with text booklets), and a round-the-clock news service focusing on Latin America. There is also a popular feature on practical medicine conducted by a physician. Listeners wishing to participate in the Friendship Chain receive a "Diploma of Friendship." Interspersed are biblical programs, usually short, that are designed to introduce Christ as "the Friend who sticks closer than a brother." Biblegrams, short Bible sayings, have the same effect as catchy tunes on the radio.

This approach has resulted in many conversions. As KGEI reviews the correspondence of listeners who are Christians, it notes that many of them originally involved themselves in KGEI's programs because of the "secular" features. Gradually they were introduced to the Lord. A good illustration is the letter from a university professor in Brazil:

> Dear Friends at the Voice of Friendship:
>
> I am a clinical psychologist, philosophy professor, and a journalist. Aside from this, for my entire life I have been a materialist, an atheist, and an admirer of Communism, both Marxist and Leninist. But now, after having heard the wonderful messages on the Voice of Friendship every night, I would like to renounce Communism and accept Jesus Christ as my personal Savior. I never attended any church and never read the Bible. I am asking you to please send me a Bible, Christian literature, and any books that will point out the errors in the Communist doctrine. Help me find salvation for my

soul through God's love. Please answer me soon for I hunger and thirst for Jesus.

I already thank you for what you will do. I would like to wish success to all my friends at the Voice of Friendship. Let me add that the literature you send me can be in Portuguese, Spanish, English, French, Italian, or German.

Respectfully yours,
Dr. F.

The walls of KGEI in San Francisco are covered with awards presented by organizations and governments showing appreciation for the work the station has done in promoting international friendship among the nations of "the hemisphere." Perhaps the most prestigious is the gold medal *Honor al Merito,* the highest award the Ministry of Communications of Paraguay can bestow on a foreign entity.

During the "Cuban crisis" the United States government commandeered KGEI for a few days to broadcast President Kennedy's messages to Latin America. FEBC President, Bob Bowman, accepted a citation for KGEI from the president at the White House.

People who have made a decision to follow Christ while listening to KGEI have been deeply influenced by the Friendship broadcasts. From time to time, new churches are started as a result of the programming. Many of these churches are established in rural areas where there is no other Christian activity of any kind. The first time KGEI received a photo of a new church building erected by the new members, a large sign on the front said, *"Iglesia de la Voz de la Amistad"* (church of the Voice of Friendship).

6

Singing Islands of the Sea

Searching for an island, the perfect island, was an awesome responsibility. Yet Manila-based Far East Broadcasting Company engineers John Wheatley and Norman Blake accepted this as their mission.

During the first eighteen years the response to the Indian language broadcasts grew to an average of two thousand letters a month from Indian listeners in central and southern India. The two Indian recording studios were Bangalore funded by Moody Institute Bible students and headed by Gordon Bell and New Delhi headed by Allen Buckwalter. These studios produced Indian broadcasts in sixteen major languages. They also coordinated programs that were contributed by missionaries and Indian Christians from seventeen organizations and denominations across India. These programs aired from the Philippines for eight and one-half hours of daily transmissions to India, Sri Lanka, Pakistan, Nepal, and Tibet.

However, Far East Broadcasting Company staff became concerned when they realized that northern India's response did not match that of central and southern India. FEBC engineers studied the impressive mountain barriers that separate northern India from southern India. They realized that the powerful shortwave signals were weakened and scattered by the mountain masses that begin to rise in northern Burma and Thailand. Ultimately these peaks reach the towering heights of the Himalayas, earning them the title, "Top of the World." They wall off the transmissions to Nepal, Bhutan, and northern India from the Philippines.

Therefore in 1962 a quest was launched for an additional transmitting site that would shoot the signal "right in the front door." This venture led John and Norman to investigate the island world in the southern part of the Indian Ocean toward northern Australia and western Indonesia. They visited Christmas Island, the Cocos, the Maldives, and other islands. Some were privately owned islands. Some islands were owned by other governments. The colorful histories and confusing laws governing radio diffusion complicated the negotiations. After five years of searching, no island met the FEBC specifications.

In Great Britain, a group headed by John's good friend, Douglas Malton, began meeting in 1959 to pray for the Wheatleys and the radio ministry. During John and Alice's first furlough home to England, the group decided to call themselves Far East Broadcasting Associates (FEBA).

In the course of his other duties, John eventually pursued the island odyssey into the Indian Ocean, where bits of protruding land are widely separated. Few are of impressive size. Most are microscopic isles, surrounded by endless expanses of water.

As the pirates of prior centuries had searched the vast waters for the perfect island to hide their stolen treasures, John searched for the place from which to give away a precious treasure of inestimable value. The finger of God seemed to push him toward a beautiful group of islands in the western Indian Ocean, isolated by a thousand miles from a continental land body—the Seychelles.

While John's steamer approached the island group, he switched his radio to Manila and heard his wife Alice wish him happy birthday. He realized that the island mass spreading before him was his birthday gift from the Lord. He had found the "perfect island." The search was over.

The Seychelles are of astounding beauty—a sprinkling of about a hundred land particles on the vast expanse of water dividing Africa from India. They are unique in the oceanic island world because most are composed of solid granite anchored to the ocean floor. Thirty-two are granitic, the rest coralline; and only a dozen are inhabited. John Wheatley's steamer took him to Mahé, the largest island measuring fifty square miles.

There, powder-fine sandy beaches scalloped the shoreline between huge granite rock piles. The land rose abruptly from the abbreviated shorelines to a height of three thousand feet. The surrounding ocean glistened mint green over coral reefs, deepening to dark blue-green as it reached out to sea.

The climate on Mahé was ideal, too. The heavy rainfall created hills of emerald velvet which were free from cyclonic winds or typhoons. Offsetting a warm and humid temperature, breezes cooled the lush green hills. But more importantly, the people were friendly and the local government was approachable. The Seychelles chain was part of the British Commonwealth at the time.

As a radio engineer John saw the island as the perfect site for broadcasting full circle to India, Sri Lanka, South Asia, Middle and Near East, and Africa. But he immediately recognized one formidable problem that had always plagued FEBC—land on which to build transmitters and antennas. In this case, level land.

In spite of the obstacles the FEBC directors decided to go ahead with the Seychelles Project in 1967. A suggestion was made that the associates in Great Britain take on the building, staffing, management, and funding of the new station. Thus was born FEBC's sister station, FEBA/Seychelles. John Wheatley became field director.

The building of the international broadcasting stations on the island of Mahé was remarkable and unique, even heroic. The team of FEBA engineers found enough land on the shoreline of the sheltered bay at Anse Etole to build a transmitter building. But because the level land around the island was minimal, the administrative buildings, production center, and staff houses were built five miles from the transmission site up a steep roadway near the town of San Souci which means "without a care." Level ground on which to build the studios had to be blasted out of granite.

The question of where to put the antenna was the next problem to overcome. There was virtually no land on this small island, but John knew God had led him there. The FEBA engineering team looked to the impossible—the sea!

Out in the warm shallow sea, anchored to the coral lying beneath, they built the most original reef aerial antenna array in the history of Christian radio. The logistics of pouring cement foundations under water were incomprehensible. FEBA engineers spent many months in rubber suits, wearing air tanks on their backs. They suspended the transmitting antennas between masts about one kilometer offshore, creating unique structures. Remote-controlled switching provided a saltwater takeoff in both directions across the ocean to the target areas. Today FEBA/Seychelles has three one hundred-thousand-watt transmitters that broadcast in twenty-five languages.

When the FEBA/Seychelles transmitters became operational in 1968, the mail soared—often to over twenty thousand letters per month. Following are letters that typify the thousands who are being drawn to the Lord Jesus Christ through radio:

I cannot express the joy I experienced listening.
Each word touched my heart. I realized that I am a sin-
ner and that I needed to be saved. I confessed my sins,
pleaded for forgiveness, and at that moment found
peace in my heart.

A listener in northern India

I received Christ as my Savior four years ago.
Three years ago persecution began, and our church was
closed. I became spiritually cold. At that time God
"split the air" to bring me your programs. Last year I
returned to the Lord.

A listener in Ethiopia

FEBA/Seychelles uses nine African languages each day,
complementing the work of local churches. Many of these
churches see radio as a helping hand, the open channel capable of assisting them to meet the needs of thousands of scattered believers and inquirers.

Acts 8:26–40 tells of Philip being sent by an angel of the
Lord to make contact with an Ethiopian eunuch, the trea-
surer of Queen Candace. Philip found the man riding in a
chariot, reading from the prophet Isaiah but not understanding what he read:

Then the Spirit said to Philip, "Go near and over-
take this chariot."
So Philip ran to him, and heard him reading the
prophet Isaiah, and said, "Do you understand what you
are reading?"
And he said, "How can I, unless someone guides
me?" And he asked Philip to come up and sit with him.
(vv. 29–31)

Philip led the Ethiopian to the Lord and baptized him.
A soldier in Mozambique was listening to the Shona lan-

guage broadcasts from FEBA/Seychelles when he wrote this encouraging letter:

> I am a soldier in the army. I am writing from Mozambique, where we are guarding the oil pipeline. I was playing with the tuner on my radio one Sunday, and I heard you speak about the God of the Bible. I stopped turning the dial and continued listening. You touched my heart. The next Sunday I invited other soldiers to listen with me. In our camp we are now many who listen to your program. Please send me a Bible in Shona. I thirst to read it every day.

Mozambique is a country slightly larger than the state of Texas. It is located on the southeast coast of Africa. Ninety percent of the people live in rural areas. Following is another letter from a Muslim in that poverty-stricken country:

> As a teenager, I first heard the gospel programs from the FEBA/Seychelles radio station using my father's radio. I listened to the Swahili service to East Africa as well as Portuguese programs broadcast to Mozambique.
>
> Soon afterwards, I became ill and visited a hospital in Tanzania. I stayed with my cousin who suggested I contact a witch doctor. However, I rejected the witch doctor's advice and spent time with Islamic teachers instead. But during that time, I could not shake off a feeling of wanting to know more about the teachings of Christ.
>
> I had experienced this when I first listened to gospel broadcasts, and it made me want to give up the ways of Islam.
>
> In your program I heard that Jesus was the Son of God. However, I knew Jesus as the prophet Issal in the Koran, and this troubled me. A man from my own

country of Mozambique had become a Christian pastor in Tanzania and knowing the Koran, he helped me to understand the difference.

I continued listening to FEBA/Seychelles, and one day I went to an open-air evangelistic meeting. There I gave my life to the Lord. I began going to church and was also healed of my neurological illness.

Later, I returned to my hometown in Mozambique and started a church that met in my home. The church soon grew, so I began organizing groups of believers around the province. I now pastor nine congregations, ministering and preaching the gospel to them.

The largest congregation now has 170 Christians, while the smallest has a group of twenty believers. The church leaders are taken through a study of the Word of God in two to three months, and each fellowship has an elder with other brothers helping. In rural communities many of the people work in the fields, so meetings are held on Saturday afternoons for those who cannot come on Sunday. I visit each congregation once a month, traveling from place to place on a bicycle given to me by friends.

When the listener wrote his first letter to FEBA/Seychelles, there were already over two hundred believers. Currently, the number exceeds five hundred. In his hometown, the congregation meets in the listener's home. He pulled down one of the mud walls to make room for worshipers. Still they cannot all get inside.

While this story is one of rejoicing, there are many hardships and insecurities of life in Mozambique. Guerilla warfare and terrorism continue to plague the country. The government, with the help of world aid agencies, struggles to stave off the effects of the economic devastation brought on by civil war. Some of the new churches are in the northern province where fighting is the fiercest. FEBC and FEBA personnel pray that these people will continue to benefit from God's protection.

The Lord builds His church by many means, not the least of which is International Missionary Radio's world outreach. There are thousands of Filipinos living and working in Saudi Arabia because work is easier to find there. Following words came to FEBC Manila from a Saudi jail:

> I'm here in Saudi Arabia where I enjoyed the "high living" with material things. But suddenly life became a nightmare, and I reached the utmost depths. I am now one of the unlucky foreigners in prison. Many of the accusations they made against me are not true. I am almost blind and helpless, and I do not understand.
>
> I believe that I am not in jail because of their charges, but condemned by God for my wrongdoings in my younger life. This is a blessing in disguise rather than a punishment. It is God's way of opening my eyes to the truth, and the truth has set me free. It has brought a complete change in my life. I have been reborn and have rediscovered myself.
>
> I attend a daily Bible study with a "congregation" composed of myself and one other prisoner. I am reminded of Matthew 18:20: "For where two or three are gathered together in My name, I am there in the midst of them."

His letter concludes:

> I will be grateful to hear from you soon. God bless you, and more power to the Far East Broadcasting Company.

Amazing! FEBC Radio has reached into prison in Riyadh, the capitol city of Saudi Arabia. This is a clear example of how missionary radio is used by God to build His Church in inaccessible places overseas.

Nepal was another example of an inaccessible place until FEBA/Seychelles launched its signal "right in the front door." Nine-tenths of Nepal lies in the world's highest mountain range, the Himalayas. The country is poor and undeveloped and has high illiteracy rate.

Brahmins form the highest caste in Hinduism, the predominant religion. They are the priests. A medical missionary from Nepal told Bob Bowman the following story regarding a young Brahmin:

> In an isolated trading town of western Nepal, the people live as they have lived for centuries. There are no proper roads, no running water, and no electricity. There was no modern medical care until the Nepalese government allowed a Christian mission to set up facilities to meet the dire physical needs of the backward Nepalese community.
>
> Previously, no Christian had ever lived there. The name of Jesus was completely unknown. The largely Brahmin community was Hindu. Idols, altars festooned with flowers and other sacrifices, and pictures of gods and goddesses were in evidence everywhere. An ornate temple stood in the middle of the marketplace.
>
> At dawn daily and again at dusk, a generator-run loudspeaker blared out the virtues of the many Hindu deities worshiped by the people. Wealthy landowners earned merit by financing the temple's loudspeaker. The tinkle of "puja bells," thought to attract the attention of the gods, was also a familiar sound in neighborhood houses.
>
> I was one of three medical missionaries placed by God into that setting. In time we trained a number of young Nepalese paramedical students to help in the

new medical center. Several became interested in the message of Jesus Christ and bought New Testaments. One of the young men had been secretly listening to the radio broadcasts for a while and had gained some understanding of the gospel. But then someone reported him to the police.

All of the medical students were called in and warned of the serious consequences if they should change religions. They were given orders to destroy their Bibles.

Although this incident generated fear, the seed of the gospel had fallen on good ground and eventually bore fruit. The medical students formed a small church.

One day an eighteen-year-old Brahmin appeared at the door of our home. He coughed several times to announce his presence. He asked a simple question, but one that required discernment in Nepal. "Is this the place where the Christians meet?"

I was aware of another incident that had happened a few months previously in a nearby town. An informer who posed as a seeker had betrayed a tiny band of Christians, and one young believer was imprisoned for a year. I wondered if the young Brahmin was sincere or sent by the authorities to spy on the Christians. I answered cautiously, "Why do you want to know? Where did you come from?"

"My name is Sashi," he said, "I come from a village eight miles distant where only Brahmins are allowed to live."

Then I asked, "How did you know of the gospel?"

The young Brahmin replied, "I have been listening to the Christian broadcasts in my home for the past two years. I started listening to the English service for the purpose of learning English. No one else in my home spoke English. Gradually I began to grasp the meaning of the message. When a Bible correspondence course was offered on the air, I wrote for it."

The young Brahmin proudly showed me the diploma he had received when he had completed the lessons and a New Testament he had received as a prize he valued. He said, "I read it several times and was persuaded that Jesus Christ is the Savior of the World. I want to become a Christian, but I am not sure how to proceed."

He had never met another Christian. However, he learned that a Christian medical mission had come to his valley, just eight miles away. And here he was at our door.

When he asked to be baptized, I explained that it could mean the loss of family, status, and future job opportunities.

It could lead to possible imprisonment.

Soon after this incident, Sashi's family sent him to college in the capital city. There he found a thriving Christian fellowship and was baptized. Today he serves the Lord in ministry.

From "singing islands," the Seychelles and the Philippines, the message of the gospel is sung daily to Asia, the Middle and Near East, East and South Africa, and the Soviet Union.

Treasure in the Yellow Sea

The small airplane's engine droned as it flew over the Yellow Sea. As he looked out the window, George Littman of the FEBC staff on Okinawa reflected on a major problem facing the organization in 1969. FEBC had met the needs of American service personnel stationed on the crowded island known as the "Isle of the August Moon" and had served the Ryukuan people on Okinawa and surrounding islands.

Just as important, they had maintained a powerful AM mediumwave voice to China off the isle's northern tip. Often staff members gathered with tears in their eyes beside the KSBU towers on a hill facing China. They prayed that the signals bearing God's love through the towers above them would comfort the hearts of those across the China Sea.

The Far East Broadcasting staff had spent twelve profitable years on Okinawa sending out the gospel. Then gradually there came an uneasiness, then the reality—Okinawa would revert to Japan. FEBC spent five years fruitlessly negotiating with the Japanese government. NHK, Nippon Broadcasting Corporation, was government controlled and could not accept a privately owned station broadcasting from its territory. It became apparent that KSBU's "Voice to China" would have to be moved off Okinawa. The question before them was, Why not find another place to build an even larger mediumwave station to China?

George pondered this problem while on vacation accompanying United States military personnel to a pheasant hunt on a popular island. Looking out the plane window, he saw a beautiful volcanic piece of land lying in the Yellow Sea eighty miles off the southwestern tip of the Korean Peninsula. Cheju-do, an island only forty miles long and twenty miles at its widest point, is sometimes called the "Hawaii of the Orient." From Mount Hanra's five-thousand-foot peak, frosted by an early snow, the land sloped gently to the sea. He caught a glimpse of a waterfall cascading through the melting snow. The water formed a stream on the flatlands that meandered through orchards of tangerines ripening in the warm autumn air.

Later at a meeting of FEBC directors, the problem of relocation surfaced again. Suddenly George recognized the value of the paradise island where he hunted—it lay two hundred and fifty miles from Shanghai. And it was four hundred miles closer to China than Okinawa. Shortly after the directors decided to explore the possibility of relocating on Cheju-do, George Littman succumbed to a congenital heart ailment and ended his earthly service to the Lord. But George had found a treasure in the Yellow Sea!

Before approaching the Korean government, David Wilkinson, FEBC Director for Japan, traveled to Korea to confer with his former college classmate, Billy Kim. When Dave asked Billy to help FEBC make the proper contacts with the Korean government, his answer was "yes," but with one stipulation. Billy had little time available because of his continually expanding Christian Service Ministry. He would work with FEBC until the government granted permission, then return to his other ministries.

As a young boy during the Korean conflict, Billy became

friends with an American GI, who sent him to the United States for an education. There he became a Christian and married a classmate named Trudy. The couple returned to Korea dedicated to reaching the people with the gospel.

Billy's ministry prospered and kept him extremely busy. His evangelism with Youth for Christ had a powerful impact on young Koreans. He became honorary chaplain of the ROK Forces and preached freely at military camps where thousands of Korean service personnel came to know the Lord. He founded a church in Suwon City that presently has a membership of over ten thousand. He and Trudy organized a hospital to meet the physical needs of their people. Billy Kim was asked to be the interpreter for the first Korean Crusade which Billy Graham conducted in the Seoul Yoido-do Plaza. His dedication to Christ and his personal integrity gained him a place of great influence in Korea. Today Billy Kim is FEBC director in Korea.

But in those days of early negotiations the contacts with the government were not easy even for Billy Kim. FEBC asked permission to build a quarter-million-watt radio station. No private broadcasting stations in Korea had that kind of power. Also, FEBC wanted permission to operate the station as an "International Voice from Korea." International broadcasting was the prerogative of the government. How would the Korean officials feel about delegating such authority to a private organization?

FEBC requested permission to broadcast to China, the Soviet Union, and North Korea, as well as Japan. Three of these nations were Communist foes of South Korea, a country constantly on guard against intrusion from North Korea. Could the South Koreans really trust FEBC?

Months of negotiation passed. With great deliberation, the South Korean government seemed to approach an affirmative conclusion. Sensing the decision was near, Dave called Bob on the phone and asked, "Mr. Bowman, are you sure that God is in this new move? It's going to take a lot of money. If the government says 'yes,' we must move quickly."

Bob replied, "Dave, I know how much it's going to cost. And I know that we don't have a dollar of it right now. If God gives us an affirmative answer from the government, He will provide."

About four in the morning Bob awakened from a restless sleep with an unsettling thought: *Where are you going to get all that money?* Yet he knew the thought was not from God because it brought doubts and uneasiness approaching panic. At 4:00 A.M. Bob's self-confidence wavered.

However he had learned that the best thing to do at these times was to get out of bed, open the Bible, and begin to read and pray. Then the Lord spoke to him. He opened his Bible to the seventy-eighth Psalm and read verse 53: "And He led them on safely, so that they did not fear." He read on in verse 72,

> So he shepherded them according
> to the integrity of his heart,
> And guided them by the
> skillfulness of his hands.

Bob's heart was reassured with a deep and abiding peace. He recalled how completely God had supplied in the past: first the vision, then the open door, and then stepping through the door—all according to His will. Perhaps the funds did not come as quickly as FEBC would have wanted, but God always provided in His time.

Bob thought back to 1963 to his first visit to South Korea. He had tried to visit Tiburcio Baja, the consul general of the Philippine Embassy in Seoul, in his office. However, Bob could not locate him. Shortly thereafter at the inauguration celebration of President Park, when the ceremonies were over and the lights came on in the cultural center auditorium, Bob discovered that the consul general stood before him.

The consul general told Bob that he had recently been called in by the government to tell what he knew about Far East Broadcasting Company. He said that the South Korean intelligence sources reported favorably on the effectiveness of the FEBC broadcasts from the Philippines on the North Koreans. The government wanted to know more about the organization.

Perhaps this was one reason why they were cordial to Far East Broadcasting Company when seven years later FEBC made application for the construction of a 250,000-watt mediumwave station on Cheju-do. In February 1971 Bob and Billy were received by the South Korean prime minister and the presidential advisor and were personally presented with the official Korean franchise to construct the powerful radio station.

Although Cheju-do seemed like the ideal place for the envisioned station, a new challenge arose. Where would they find a sizable piece of land on a small rural farming island?

The easiest way to survey the island was by air. The ROK Air Force volunteered the use of a helicopter. Norman Blake located an ideal site on the China side of the shoreline about eight miles west of Cheju's main city, near the airport. Facing toward China along the shoreline, it was perfect from the standpoint of position and provided a great saltwater "take-off path" directly to China and Russia. Saltwater is the best known conductor of radio waves. Nearness to the airport would simplify the transportation of needed supplies as the construction began.

Meanwhile, back at the headquarters office in California, FEBC executives were concerned about the sixty-thousand-dollar price for the land. How would God provide it?

Once again FEBC was the beneficiary of a unique, unselfish gesture by three other radio ministries. These ministries learned about the project and the need for money to purchase the acreage. "Back To the Bible Broadcast," "The Haven of Rest," and "The Chapel of the Air" agreed that they would combine efforts to raise the funds from their missionary-minded audiences. Each of them set aside a missionary month on their broadcasts to talk about the new Cheju-do station. Almost twice the amount asked for was donated, providing funds not only to purchase the land, but also to begin construction on the needed buildings.

At a conference in Seoul soon thereafter, David Wilkinson slumped to the floor as a massive brain tumor claimed his life. Sadly, FEBC had lost another director in little more than a year.

Yet the vision continued to be carried on. Workers poured huge cement foundations for the towers. Houses were built of concrete to withstand the typhoons that move through the Yellow Sea.

Then suddenly, a United States Agency for International Development (AID) agent, who was an advisor to the Korean government, saw the building taking place and asked questions. When he found out that Far East Broadcasting Company was building a quarter-million-watt radio station, he became agitated.

The man wrote a letter of protest to the Korean government stating concern that such a powerful station would wipe out the radio instrument landing service at the Cheju airport just five miles away. He recommended that the government issue a "cease-work order" until a study could be made.

FEBC engineers had already discussed this possibility

with the government authorities. Their study showed that there was no problem, but the AID man was not convinced. The South Korean government asked that work be stopped for a further study.

Meanwhile, negotiations were taking place with a large transmitter building company in the United States for transmitter construction. FEBC was ready to sign a contract when word came of the stop order on Cheju-do. They decided not to sign the transmitter contract until it could be determined whether the project would proceed.

A newspaper man, after learning of FEBC's proposed station, published an article in the *London Daily Telegraph*. An executive of a transmitter company in Switzerland read the article and immediately contacted the FEBC office in California.

"We read of your project. We have a 250,000-watt-mediumwave transmitter on the production line. It is the last model for this year. After it is finished we will retool our plant for next year's model. We will give you a special price on it." During the next three weeks a price that provided a large saving to FEBC was agreed upon.

In the middle of FEBC's negotiations with the Swiss company, the Korean government decided that the study showed no problem and that construction could proceed. Amazing! God's "stop orders" are often as important as His "go signals." By waiting three weeks FEBC saved over a hundred thousand dollars on the purchase price.

The transmitter and other electronic equipment arrived from Switzerland and were stored in the customs warehouse awaiting the high customs payment of $499 thousand. There was no money in the bank to pay that amount, and after one year the Korean customs office said the cargo must be cleared immediately or go up for auction.

Billy and H. K. Kim, the chairman of the Korean FEBC

board, visited the prime minister to ask for clearance. They submitted petitions to multiple offices and again visited the prime minister and the minister of culture and information.

Soon a cable from Billy Kim arrived at Far East Broadcasting headquarters in California. It contained one word: "Hallelujah!" The transmitter had been freed from customs and was on its way to Cheju-do. God had answered their prayer.

On March 8 the transmitter arrived in forty crates that were immediately loaded on trucks and brought to the site. Eleven FEBC engineers converged from several countries. The delay of the arrival of the transmitter had eaten into their two-year construction permit. If the station was not on the air by May 31, the permit would be lost.

There was an air of expectancy as the engineers opened the crates. Forty wooden boxes labeled with international symbols, arrows, umbrellas, and goblets showed no indication of what was inside or what should go where. The FEBC engineers had installed large transmitters for Okinawa, Christian Radio City Manila, and Bocaue in the Philippines, and a 250,000-watt transmitter for KGEI in San Francisco. Yet upon opening the crates, they froze with dismay. What they saw was a "do-it-yourself" transmitter! The front panel was twenty-five feet long and ten feet wide with many components, and it came in "parts to assemble." There were four books of instructions—all written in German. The engineers had anticipated a totally constructed transmitter disassembled at a minimum for shipping. Lew Entz was one of the engineers who felt God had called him. He volunteered and came from Iowa at his own expense. He arrived on Cheju-do shortly before the transmitter was delivered. He was the only person who could read the German instructions.

Lew said, "Normally Swiss engineers do the installations, so that's why the instructions were in German. I began

(Left) Bob and Eleanor Bowman in 1946—committed to the venture.
(Right) John and Dorothy Broger in 1946—starting the first eventful year with the Bowmans.

Bob sees John off for China in 1946. They had $1,000 and a vision.

Bob and John broadcasting on FEBC's first radio station, DZAS, in the Philippines in 1946.

FEBC's first station goes on the air at Christian Radio City in Manila in June 1948.

Bob behind the microphone in 1949 at Christian Radio City, Manila. Soon the ideal of the national speaking his heart-language to his own people would be realized.

Hundreds of the "portable missionaries," or the "boxes that can talk," are made and distributed throughout the Philippines.

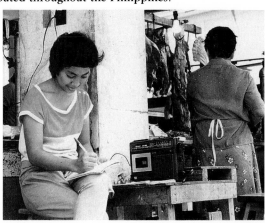

Radio is a teacher as well as a preacher. In the Philippine marketplace, a listener can study a Bible correspondence course.

Efren Palorina manages the Philippine stations. Only 10 percent of FEBC's 854 full-time staff are from the West.

President of the Philippines, Corazon Aquino, with Dr. Bowman and the FEBC Director of the Philippines, Fred Magbanua. In 1990, Mrs. Aquino congratulated FEBC on its 40th anniversary and made a national proclamation honoring its work.

FEBC recording studios and administration buildings in Seoul, South Korea.

FEBC's U.S. headquarters and recording studios building in La Mirada, California.

KGEI antenna beside San Francisco Bay transmits the gospel to all of South America and over the North Pole into all eleven time zones of the Soviet Union.

When the *glasnost* window opened in 1990, Russian listeners were invited to write directly to FEBC, P.O. Box 1, La Mirada, CA. Hundreds of letters poured in daily, as many as 4,840 in a single month.

Dr. Bowman talks to young Chinese students in Tiananmen Square in 1985. Many Chinese said they heard of Christ through FEBC's Chinese broadcasts, which started in 1949. In China, 95 percent of the people listen to radio.

FEBA/Seychelles engineers built unique antennas in the sea on coral beds. These transmit powerful signals to India, the Near and Middle East, and East and South Africa.

Natives listen to the gospel in their own language in Indonesia. FEBC broadcasts in 120 languages.

FEBC Vietnamese broadcasters: on the Communist "hit list," they escaped Vietnam on one of the last planes out before their country was overrun by Communist forces. Now they send the message of hope back to their people.

Through the influence of FEBC radio, Lee Chong's whole village in Laos came to Christ when he was eight years old. Now he broadcasts in the Hmong language to his own country.

Marpi Cliff in Saipan is one of the most strategic spots in the world for international shortwave broadcasting.

Over 8,000 pieces of WWII unexploded ammunition had to be removed from Marpi Cliff by brave FEBC personnel before building could be started.

Roy Alvarez checks the tape and cassette automation control on Saipan.

Two of five powerful transmitters in Marpi Cliff, Saipan, that send signals to China and across Russia.

Tape library on Saipan. Thousands of recorded programs are needed for FEBC's 300 program hours of daily broadcasts.

to interpret some words like 'weld this' and 'saw this,' 'cut this to fit here.'

"Another confusing thing was that although there were thousands of parts, the numbers were rarely above one hundred. Several unrelated parts had the same number. It was extremely confusing, and I prayed desperately about it for two days.

"Throughout the instructions the word 'rubic' kept reoccurring. I could not find it in my German vocabulary. Finally I decided it meant 'option.' They gave us as many as four parts to serve one function on the transmitter.

"Transmitters usually come with the wires cut and wired together with terminals, and you simply lay the harness in and fasten the wires at both ends. It took a long time for the truth to soak in—they had simply sent spools of wire!

"I realized that these parts had never been assembled and the transmitter had never been tested. In fact, some of the parts came from Austria, some from Great Britain, and the bulk from Switzerland. The Swiss company normally installed the transmitters themselves with their own crews. They had sent materials with which you can build a transmitter instead of an already built one."

Each FEBC engineer worked in his own area of expertise to raise six 184-foot towers. Crews of ten to fifteen Cheju women were hired to pull ropes at the bottom of a pulley—a "gin" pole method that used a thirty-foot pole to raise the towers a section at a time.

The Swiss company requested notification of the air date so that they could supervise placing the station on the air. But when they received the first cable that Cheju-do was scheduled to go on the air, they did not believe it. They ignored it. The second cable stated, "If you want to see HLAZ go on the air, you better come now!"

A representative of the Switzerland company arrived

and spent six days going over the work. It only took two days to correct the errors made in putting the transmitter together. The Swiss representative stated that it normally took two years to accomplish what had been done on Cheju-do in those three months. He was not aware of such an achievement in any other circumstance in the world. Testing the new powerful equipment was usually done slowly, cautiously, over a period of a year. They had met a humanly impossible deadline, but with God nothing is impossible.

Engineers are an extremely valuable and rare breed of missionary. Without men of this calling, FEBC signals would not be circling the earth.

These men are not noticed at ceremonies and celebrations. They are more often found covered with grime and sweat, hidden behind pieces of electronic equipment while they solve problems. Engineers live in an esoteric electrical world: tubes, filaments, and mysterious calculations of ionospheres and sunspots. These Christian missionaries often refuse lucrative secular jobs, which their educations and abilities qualified them for.

These men also possess perseverance. Daily they face unique problems. Their outposts are usually far from the electronics parts suppliers. They fill out request forms, send them across the sea, and wait. Sometimes the powerful electronic giants they work on are beyond their training, and they often have to work with inadequate tools.

Far East Broadcasting Company engineers also face problems peculiar to their locations. They have to contend with rats chewing wires, dust and sand blowing into delicate equipment, flood damage, and mildew. Other problems arise from tropical heat, typhoons, and the extreme danger involved in working with powerful electricity. The FEBC engineers were tried to the limits of their fortitude on Cheju-do. But their reward was in the realization that those in distant places would learn of Jesus Christ because of their dedication and perseverance.

June 30, 1973, was a day of jubilee when the new Cheju-do transmitting site was dedicated to the glory of God. Many government dignitaries and foreign visitors were there. "Open Door to China: Phase I" became operational. At that point a new more powerful voice in the AM mediumwave band came on the air to China capable of reaching the tiniest $3.75 radio receiver. At last those who owned an AM radio could listen to the gospel of Christ in China as easily as those who had shortwave receivers.

However, the HLAZ potential audience is not limited to China. The broadcasts are heard daily in the USSR across the Ural Mountains into Moscow adding another 250 million within its coverage area. Early test transmissions to Japan revealed that HLAZ could be heard from southern Japan to the northernmost parts of Hokkaido Island.

North Korea is one of the two most tightly closed nations in the Communist orbit. Evidence of HLAZ's potential effectiveness in the Korean language came a few days after the dedication ceremony. North Korea's Radio Pyongyang loudly protested the "powerful station" set up on Cheju-do to "disrupt the thinking" of the North Korean people. FEBC hoped the loving presentation of the gospel would reach the hearts of the North Koreans too.

A few months later the magnitude of what God had accomplished dawned upon Far East Broadcasting Company personnel. The Lord had placed HLAZ in the most strategic spot in the world where 1.2 billion people lived within the nighttime coverage of its signal! One-quarter of the entire world population lay within the reach of a single powerful AM transmitter broadcasting from Cheju-do.

Bob Bowman traveled to Korea and met with the prime minister, who said, "We wish that we could have the effect on our surrounding nations out there that Far East Broadcasting Company is having, Dr. Bowman, but politically it is not possible."

One morning in his hotel room beside the Han River, Bob awakened to the sound of church bells ringing out across Seoul. It was 4:30 A.M., and although this was not Sunday, Christians were going to Church for an hour of prayer. Worshiping before work was a regular occurrence. The bells chimed:

> Rock of ages, cleft for me,
> Let me hide myself in Thee;
> Let the water and the blood,
> From Thy wounded side which flowed,
> Be of sin the double cure,
> Save from wrath and make me pure.

In Bob's own words:

> The depth of the meaning of those hymns had never struck me as forcefully as on that morning. The first faint rays of early dawn crept across the landscape eerily beautiful. Against the backdrop of Korea's mountains, the lacelike mist enshrouded the Land of the Morning Calm. And I said, "Dear Korea, you've not always known the peace that hovers over the city this morning. The meaning of your call to prayer is real as you face the constant danger of attack from the North." I realized that the North's jet fighter planes sat ready sixty seconds away.

Another hymn rang out from the steeples. Long after the chimes had called hundreds of thousands of Korean Christians to prayer, Bob sat deep in thought.

The Land of the Morning Calm has known the sorrow of loved ones lost in deadly conflict. South Koreans were harassed by international news media and politicians alike over alleged lack of religious freedom and human rights. Yet here was a land that had granted FEBC the freedom to broadcast the gospel of Christ from her shores, with no strings attached, reaching one-quarter of the human race.

8

Escape from Vietnam

"We don't know what our future will be. Things change so quickly." Tears, unbidden, rose in Nguyen Thi's eyes as he spoke these words to Bob Bowman.

How could Bob answer the young FEBC staff member? The tense atmosphere around the Tan Son Nhut Airport in Saigon added to his awkwardness as Bob greeted his beloved colleagues. They settled into a car with Chaplain Nguyen Ba Quang for the ride to the Caravelle Hotel on a sultry March day in 1975.

That evening sixty people gathered at the FEBC office in Saigon. Hoang Bich, director of the Far East Broadcasting Company's Saigon studio, was the wife of Chaplain Quang. The group consisted of Vietnamese pastors and their wives, a few missionaries, and the FEBC Vietnamese staff.

The atmosphere of the meeting with these Vietnamese Christians was surprisingly calm considering that their country was making its last struggle for freedom. They received word that the Communists of the North had liquidated ten thousand refugees on the road leading from one highland city by spraying them with gunfire. A Japanese newspaper estimated the death count at fifty thousand.

Bich turned to Bob and asked, "Dr. Bowman, will you say a few words to us?" Bob felt totally inadequate under the circumstances. Some of those seated around him, including the FEBC staff, were high on a North Vietnam Communist hit list that South Vietnamese intelligence had intercepted. He knew these dedicated people were aware of the threat hanging over them.

After a moment's pause, Bob shared Matthew 6:25–27:

Therefore I say to you, do not worry about your life, what you will eat or what you will drink; nor about your body, what you will put on. Is not life more than food and the body more than clothing?

Look at the birds of the air, for they neither sow nor reap nor gather into barns; yet your heavenly Father feeds them. Are you not of more value than they?

The pastor who headed the Evangelical Church of Vietnam responded, "Whether in life or in death, we will be faithful to our Lord Jesus."

One young pastor told the story of how years before he had seen his Christian father murdered by the Communists. The soldiers arrived at his home late one night and demanded that his father get out of bed. He was beheaded in front of his wife and son. Many other atrocities performed by the Vietcong were related that evening.

The next morning the Quang and Thi families joined Bob for breakfast at the hotel. The meal sat untouched as they discussed the options before them. They knew that God must be trusted to get the staff out of Saigon as quickly as possible.

Suddenly Bich leaned over the table and whispered to Bob, "Spies!" The waiter was trying to hear Bob's words and to see what he wrote in his notebook.

Leaving their breakfast uneaten, they went to Bob's fifth-floor room for more privacy. As they entered, the same waiter appeared in the doorway directly across the hall. French doors with louvers let sound travel from one room to the next. The Vietcong were everywhere. And no one knew whom to trust.

A few days before when Bob attended the annual Field Director's Conference in Manila, an American woman handed him her brother's card and suggested that he might be able to help FEBC in some way. Bob hoped to locate the man in Saigon although he realized it might be impossible.

On Bob's second day in Saigon, however, the Quangs took him to the International Church. Bob prayed for a contact who would lead to the staff's evacuation. As the service ended, he noticed an American gentleman walking down the church steps. The two men greeted one another and exchanged cards. Bob stared at the same business card he had received in Manila. Then he realized that his contact was a United States government man and the answer to his prayer.

That afternoon, Le Van Thai, an elderly Vietnamese pastor, came to Bob's hotel with an urgent message. "In these difficult times, radio takes on greater importance for my people. I am willing to risk my life to get out of Vietnam in order to give my people the comfort they need. They can receive it only by radio!"

Until 1954 the eighty-year-old pastor had headed the church in North Vietnam. When Ho Chi Minh urged him to start a "National Salvation Movement," he was not willing to compromise his Lord so he went to South Vietnam. The dedicated pastor later escaped to the United States and worked as an advisor for the FEBC Vietnamese staff and the Vietnamese churches until his death.

When Bob had rearranged his schedule to stop in Saigon, he had not yet realized the urgency of the situation. He could stay only twenty-six hours. But once he arrived, he knew the FEBC staff needed to exit South Vietnam.

Three possibilities were available. The staff could try to leave through legal emigration channels; they could attempt a clandestine passage on a boat on the chance of reaching a neutral country; or perhaps it might be arranged to place them on a list at the United States Embassy for possible air evacuation. Yet no one knew if such a list existed.

Bob flew to Hong Kong and placed an urgent telephone call to Carl Lawrence who was then FEBC general program director in the Philippines. "Carl, I think we can forget that program seminar you expect to hold in Saigon in two weeks. Vietnam is on the way down and won't last much longer." Bob continued, "I'm asking you to take the earliest plane possible out of Manila and get over there. But first stop by Hong Kong to pick up the business card and letter I have for you. We must get our people out. I've made one contact whom you might be able to use as a starter."

Within hours Carl reached Saigon. Realizing the situation, he called Eric Parsons, FEBC director in Thailand, and requested that he come. Prayerfully they worked together on the grave problem.

It was soon evident that emigration channels were impossible. In an attempt to keep the morale of the soldiers high and to avoid panic, the South Vietnamese government decreed that all male citizens were prohibited from leaving the country. Exit visas for women were also suspended. Besides that, FEBC representatives were informed, "Every other clerk in the immigration office is a Vietcong. No chance."

Plan two was put into action. They booked a vessel and scheduled to set sail out of Saigon Harbor at a propitious moment. The boat would have to evade the gunboats in the Mekong Delta successfully. This was a dangerous and highly questionable means of escape. If the boat cleared the Mekong Delta, the open seas offered greater peril. Countless refugees lost their lives on the merciless, uncertain waters.

April 17 was the date set for sailing. On April 18 Far East Broadcasting Company headquarters in California received a cable from Saigon requesting prayer. It stated that the boat had cleared Saigon Harbor and was headed through the Mekong Delta with a load of two hundred refugees.

On April 21 another cable reported, "Entire 'cargo' intercepted on Mekong. Total manifest incarcerated Saigon." Tragedy gripped the worldwide FEBC family. On the other side of the world, however, the Vietnamese staff was concerned about an entirely different matter. They had missed the boat! When the staff arrived by car at the harbor, they found that the boat had left its first embarkation point. They sped toward the spot where a second rendezvous with the boat was to take place. On the way, Chaplain Quang's car suddenly developed fuel pump problems, and they missed the boat again by fifteen minutes.

The carload sat stunned beside the empty dock. Had their last means of escape just sailed away? Then, Nguyen Ai spoke up prophetically. "That wasn't a very dignified way to go anyhow. God is going to fly us out!"

With a sense of resignation, they went back to the place where they were staying together and hoped for word from the United States Embassy. Without that word, certain death faced them.

Additional contacts with congressmen, senators, state department officials in Washington, and the United States Army chief of chaplains, General Gerhardt Hyatt, were made by FEBC's United States office. They made every effort to get the Vietnamese staff on the evacuation list. FEBC's executive director, Dr. Eugene Bertermann, spent entire days contacting officials. He reported a great sense of cooperation from all with whom he spoke.

Days passed. April 23, 1975, one week before Vietnam fell, the FEBC staff dispersed to their various homes to await the inevitable. Previously they had stayed together at Chaplain Quang's home awaiting a possible call from the United States Embassy. Saigon was in a turmoil of panic, rumors, and desperate plots for escape. Fear paralyzed most people, but Chaplain Quang and the FEBC staff were filled with the peace that comes with prayerful submission to God's will.

At 4:00 P.M., one hour after the others had gone home, a messenger arrived at Quang's house with a sealed message: "Pastor Quang, have all your people ready at 5:00 P.M. at the following address. Speak to no one about this."

Quang sent rapid phone calls and messengers out and was able to reach all of them but the Nguyen Thi family and a single woman, Toan. The Thi family finally received Quang's message at 5:00 P.M. Nevertheless they quickly hailed a taxi, hoping that the pickup at the appointed place might be delayed. Their hearts pounded as their taxi pushed its way through Saigon's teeming streets toward the meeting point.

Toan had started home through downtown Saigon. Miraculously, among the thousands of bicycle riders in the crowded street, someone in the taxi spotted the missing Toan! The taxi stopped, and they called to her. Leaving her bike by the curbside, she climbed into the car. She took nothing with her but her purse.

Meanwhile, Chaplain Quang had prevailed upon the team from the United States Embassy to wait until 5:30 P.M.

At exactly that time the taxi arrived with the missing FEBC staff members. From the rendezvous point, three embassy sedans with diplomatic license plates transported them through the city, past checkpoints, to the American military terminal at the airport. Soon they were safely aboard a huge United States C-46 aircraft bound for Clark Air Force Base, Philippines, along with NBC, CBS, and ABC news journalists.

The United States news reporters stared curiously at the little band of Vietnamese as they settled in their seats. "Who are you?" one asked diminutive Mrs. Minh Thi.

"We are FEBC," she replied proudly. The entire Vietnam staff flew out on one of the last planes to leave Tan Son Nhut Airport. Not one individual was lost.

As Quang led his group to the reception desk at Clark Air Force Base and identified himself, he was greeted by the receptionist: "Praise the Lord! We've been expecting you."

On April 23 at Far East Broadcasting Company headquarters in Southern California, the telephone rang. The voice of Carl Lawrence from Manila said, "Listen carefully." Then the FEBC Manila staff joined him singing. "Let's just praise the Lord, praise the Lord. . . ." Carl's voice continued, "That's our way of telling you that our Vietnamese staff members have arrived safely at Clark Field."

Later they found that Pastor Nguyen Ba Quang, his wife and family, and Far East Broadcasting Company Vietnamese staff were number two on a Communist hit list because of their years of gospel broadcasting to that war-ravaged country. God delivered them shortly before the nation's fall.

Today their daily broadcasts are taped in the La Mirada, California, office. Since God brought them from the land of their birth, they have not missed one day of broadcasting to their homeland. Their voices and messages are the "balm of

Gilead" poured out on the weary, troubled people of present day Vietnam.

The Vietnam conflict had raged through tropical heat, humidity, and the monsoons of Southeast Asia. Day after day, discouraged American soldiers and their Vietnamese allies faced exhausting battles with the baffling Vietcong. Whether confronted with single snipers or entire battalions, they daily fought a life-or-death battle.

By night the weary troops struggled against swarms of mosquitoes, depression, and relentless loneliness that never left their sweltering tents. Many soldiers heard words of hope broadcast across the South China Sea from FEBC's Manila transmitters. The gentle, peaceful message of Jesus Christ filled the voids of despair in their hearts. In the midst of conflict, spiritual triumphs quietly took place, day after day, night after night. But still the chilling reality of the Vietnam conflict continued, taking a great toll in human lives.

Three words formed the ideals expressed by the Socialist Republic of Vietnam as the Communists took over the country in 1975: independence, freedom, and happiness. These were the exact values the people of Vietnam lost in the process.

Soon, as predicted by elderly pastor Le Van Thai, radio was the only way to reach the people of Vietnam. Reports trickled in through escaping boat people and by other means even though the flow of letters had temporarily dried up.

A visitor at the La Mirada headquarters looked at a folder of recently received letters from Vietnam and asked, "How much does it cost to mail a letter to FEBC from Vietnam today?"

Pastor Quang replied, "About half a month's wages."

Despite the cost, letters now arrive bearing joyous messages:

My dearest friends,

I was born into God's family about a year ago. Since then, my life has been changed, not only through God's Word, but also through temptations and sufferings. Because of His love I have been encouraged in times of trial and comforted in times of sorrow. Every time I listen to your teaching of God's Word in the broadcasts, my heart is filled with joy. I pray that the Lord will continue to use you in a mighty way, so that many more will hear and be saved.

Two hundred Vietnamese tribesfolk belonging to the FULRO-Dega movement crossed into Thailand and told Thai authorities that radio broadcasts from FEBC kept their hopes alive while they were in Vietnam. The tribal service from FEBC to Vietnam included twenty-three dialects. Most of the programs aired were Bible readings produced by the Summer Institute of Linguistics (SIL).

A village in North Vietnam near the China border began listening to the FEBC broadcasts in the Nung language. Eight hundred were converted to Christianity. They sent a representative to Hanoi and met with a leader of the registered church. They requested a pastor, but were given only a Bible and a songbook which they still use today.

Another letter recently arrived in La Mirada from that same village. The Christians now number over two thousand. They have five churches, but they still have no pastor, only deacons who faithfully listen to FEBC to receive spiritual food and instruction to minister to their congregations. They recently sent two young men to Hanoi Bible School to train for the ministry.

Besides the high cost of postage stamps, the response to religious broadcasting can be life endangering if such correspondence falls into the wrong hands. The risks are immense. Still they write.

From Ho Chi Minh City:

> It was a great joy when I listened to your broadcast the first time. When my country fell into Communist control, I was not a Christian yet. After going through a rough and difficult time, I finally accepted Christ as my Savior. However, I did not have much opportunity to study God's Word and grow in the faith. For by that time, most of the pastors had been imprisoned. One day a friend told me about FEBC broadcasts, and now I can listen to God's Word every evening.

From Dong-nai:

> Although my friends have left me, I still listen to your programs and pray for you every day. Because my desire is to bring the gospel message to everyone, I do not keep your broadcasts to myself. I turn the volume of my radio to maximum, then connect it to a loudspeaker so that everyone in the neighborhood can hear.

This man was recently arrested by the local Communists. From an unidentified Vietnamese village:

> I am in danger of being put into a concentration camp. I am afraid that this letter is the last one I will write to you. If so, I send my warmest greetings to all of you, and thank you for sending me the precious literature in the past. Being a Christian here, the persecution can come any time. I do not know what they will do to me, either going to the camp or losing my job. However, in God I have put my trust, and He will protect me from all evil plans. Please pray for me.

Today, members of the evacuated FEBC Vietnamese staff are still at the organization's La Mirada, California, international headquarters. They talk constantly about new and better ways to minister to those they left behind. And they pray—for those they remember and for those who write.

They know that God brought them out for a purpose. In life or in death, the victims of Vietnam's tragic history must not be forgotten.

9

Revolution of Love

A bright moon, sweeping across the starry midnight sky, washed over the transmitter buildings of Christian Radio City Manila with a dim white light. It picked out the figure of a guard as he passed between inky pools of tree shade, his torch darting in the blackness like stabs of summer lightning.

Colored monitor lights on several transmitters showed through the windows. Technicians worked late into the night on a new transmitter inside the building.

In the stillness, night sounds carried across the heavy atmosphere with astounding clarity. The footsteps of an announcer crackled on the gravel as he walked along the roadway between the quieted compound houses. The muted sounds of gospel broadcasting in unfamiliar tongues filtered into the night air. The operator checked the overseas schedules to make certain the message of Jesus Christ kept rendezvous with listeners near and far.

Behind the night-hushed scene stood a tall antenna tower, pinnacled by red warning lights. At the top, a man held by his head dangled helplessly three hundred feet from the ground!

Fred Magbanua, director of Far East Broadcasting Company, Philippines, later described this fateful moment:

> Ten thousand watts of radio frequency current was burning me alive! My head felt like it was locked in a vice held precariously in an electromagnetic field.
> *Is this death?* I wondered. Then, through the sparking and arcing, I heard my own voice saying, "I beseech you therefore, brethren, by the mercies of God, that you present your bodies a living sacrifice . . ." I realized that my own program was going out over the antenna, and my head, locked by the radio frequency power, was acting as a conductor. As I lost consciousness, I cried, "Lord, I commend to You my spirit." Then I fell.
> I regained consciousness a few moments later eight feet below. My leg caught on a brace, saving me from a deadly fall to the ground. A fuse blew, causing my release. A few seconds more and I would have burned to death.

Dazed and seriously injured, Fred miraculously descended the open ladder alone, fearing each step would be his last. God kept him conscious till he reached the ground and somehow staggered to the compound nurse's home. He was rushed to the hospital in almost unbearable pain, his head severely burned. A dozen deep holes, the largest four inches in diameter, had burned like charcoal clear to the skull. X rays showed a black spot on his brain.

Hundreds of Christians prayed for him. After three months in the hospital, the X rays showed no brain damage. The healing was complete.

During his recovery, Fred had plenty of time to think. As a young child growing up in Negros Province in a traditional Philippine religion, he never knew what it meant to receive

Christ into his heart personally. As a young boy during World War II, he saw bombs, fear, and death everywhere. Then shortly after the war ended, he heard FEBC stations and longed to know Jesus Christ and not to fear death.

He accepted Jesus as his personal Savior and wanted to go to Bible school, but his family needed his financial help. So he studied to be a civil engineer. He also determined to serve his Savior. He joined a team that went from village to village preaching the gospel. It was then that he met Aliw, a girl with a beautiful singing voice.

Aliw possessed Christian maturity beyond her years. When she was six, her family lived in a rural province of the Philippines. Her village, like others, was continually terrorized by Communist raids, the Japanese army, and the sudden appearance of Philippine guerillas. Her beloved father, mayor of their village, was taken away by the Japanese, never to return. The family fled, hiding along dangerous roadways.

In those years of growing up, Aliw's character developed under the need to help her mother and family survive financially. Becoming a Christian was not a light decision. She determined to serve the Lord with her life. She wanted to marry a minister, but Fred was an engineer.

Nevertheless, they married. Fred pastored a small church but soon realized that he needed more Bible training. He enrolled in the Far Eastern Bible Institute next door to FEBC's radio station in Manila and began working for FEBC as an engineer and broadcaster.

Temptation came, as it frequently does, in a legitimate form. A letter from an old classmate arrived from the United States urging him to accept an engineering job with high starting pay.

He read the letter to his wife. Aliw was not impressed. "I don't care how good the salary is. You made a promise to the Lord never to take a job that was not connected with spreading the gospel."

"We could support pastors with that extra money," Fred explained. But Aliw would not agree. That night when Fred went to the station to record his program, he decided to write an acceptance for the job anyway and tell his wife later. Fred continued to describe what happened that night:

> My program was a message on Romans 12:1 and 2. I left the recorded program with the operator. As I started to leave the compound I noticed the burned-out warning light on the top of the antenna. This was dangerous and had to be changed. I threw the ground switch, not realizing the high voltage wasn't effectively grounded. Then I climbed the three-hundred-foot tower.
>
> "Fred," God seemed to say, "You were telling others to surrender their lives to Me, but you yourself were trying to run away to New York to better yourself."

On the hospital bed, Fred renewed his promise to God never to take a job that was not connected with spreading the gospel. He said, "It is a fearful thing to fall into the hands of the Living God!"

Today Fred Magbanua, as managing director of Far East Broadcasting Company, Philippines, has the responsibility for FEBC's oldest operation. With a staff of over two hundred, FEBC Manila is responsible for twenty-one domestic and overseas broadcasting stations in the Philippines that have signals fanning out to cover all of Asia.

FEBC has labored in a partnership of love with the Republic of the Philippines for forty-five years. It was given permission to broadcast by the new government within days of the forming of the republic in 1945.

The Philippine government has allowed FEBC to expand over the years. The succession of presidents from Quirino to the present (including Presidents Garcia, Magsaysay, and Marcos) have graciously commended the organization. President Cory Aquino congratulated Far East Broadcasting Company on its fortieth anniversary on the air in June 1988 and invited five hundred FEBC staff and friends to Malacanyang Palace. President Aquino proclaimed the first week in June of every year as National Gospel Broadcast Week in the Philippines, under the auspices of Far East Broadcasting Company. President Aquino stated:

> It is my pleasure to join Far East Broadcasting Company in celebrating its fortieth anniversary as a noncommercial and Christian radio broadcasting network. Few other institutions can claim the satisfaction of four decades of unceasing labor to promote friendship and understanding in the world. FEBC's varied programs and inspirational messages beamed in seventy languages and dialects to Asia have done much to instill a sense of community among diverse people and cultures.
>
> I welcome the renewed commitment of FEBC to the ministry of Christian love and reconciliation. For no other message can be as effective in removing mutual doubts and suspicions that have stood in the way of peace and harmony between nations.
>
> FEBC has been a good friend to the Filipino people, and we hope it will remain so in the years ahead.
>
> Corazon C. Aquino

The 1986 Philippine government's "Revolution of Love" provided a great opportunity for FEBC to reach the entire Philippine nation at one time with God's Word. During the crisis FEBC tied all its Philippine domestic stations together in a network with a capacity to reach the fifty-five million people of the Philippines twenty-four hours a day. One international shortwave station was added to give a voice to the world beyond the Republic.

Director Magbanua invited pastors from Manila to help "man the microphones" together with the company staff. The pastors interspersed appropriate passages from the Bible with prayer and a call to national repentance every hour on the hour. They opened six telephone lines to the listeners, inviting them to ask any questions that the pastors might answer. In the first forty-eight hours, nearly six thousand calls were received.

Listening to FEBC became the focal point of the traumatized population throughout the islands as it became evident that these stations were the only source of objective news available. Many commercial radio stations throughout the Philippines began rebroadcasting the FEBC network in its effort to bring the nation to prayer.

After the crisis some commercial managers reflected that it was the first time in history that their stations had Bible reading and prayer every hour on the hour.

On the second morning, a contingent of constabulary troops arrived at Christian Radio City Manila and politely asked permission to come through the gates. They stayed on the compound until the crisis was over, but they never interfered with the broadcasts. Later FEBC learned that the troops were sent by General Fidel Ramos, the new secretary of defense.

The general was very aware of FEBC. On the thirtieth anniversary of broadcasting, he had sent a message as the chief of the constabulary troops. In it he said:

> The pioneering work done by Far East Broadcast-
> ing Company, Philippines in preaching the Gospel

through the medium of the radio has been experienced by millions of people for the last thirty years. It has made them conscious and acutely aware of the precepts and doctrines of Christianity. And this has contributed much to the improved conditions of peace and order in our land.

On the northern shore of Luzon Island in Zambales Province is the little-known city of Iba. Phase II of Open Door to China was built there by Far East Broadcasting Company to continue the circle of love to China. A 250-thousand-watt mediumwave station, DWRF, was dedicated in 1975.

Building the Iba station was never an easy job. The bumpy road from Manila wound over and around mountains, through banana groves and small barrios, and along the seashore. It took five and one-half hours to reach Iba from Manila. Radio stations need to be built where there is plenty of area to stretch antenna, and they need the right takeoff spot for the signals, preferably salt water.

The building of the station demanded the utmost in physical endurance from the engineers. Leaving their homes and families in Manila temporarily, they worked in heat, surrounded by insects. They lived in a small nipa accommodation they called the "Iba Hilton." Byrd Brunemeier wrote a poem summing up their joy and exaltation when the work was done. It is titled "It Is Finished—It Is Begun":

It is finished.
The hacking of trails through jungle undergrowth;
The bamboo, the thorns, the hot coral;
The awareness that our drama is being staged in God's
    own amphitheater;
The hush of rose-tinted dawn, rising up behind the
    ranges;
The withering impact of noonday sun;

The stunning gilt-red sunset, stretched across the sea;
The mellow lavender afterglow, dissolving into black;
The gleaming gem of Venus, suspended on the night;
The murmur of the fitful surf, washing starlit dunes;
The survey of the land, probing and peering through the canopy of greens;
The groundbreaking, the laying of foundations;
The rising of scaffolding and then the walls;
The spirited debating at meal time;
The pungent missionary humor that laughs where others might curse;
The battle of the wire plow with primeval jungle roots;
The rising of six towers against the sky;
The arrival of electric power, the novel of lights at night;
The humming of transformers and the thrumming of blowers;
The throwing of switches and the glowing of tubes;
The clatter of overload relays, the sudden smoke and charred components;
The wonder—the questions—the perplexity;
The assurance that God is there;
The improvising, the makeshift remedies;
The first test broadcast on the China beam;
The regular broadcasts to Indochina;
The full broadcast schedule.
For the builder, it is finished.

The voice of God speaks from Iba;
It has begun.
The voice of God speaks forgiveness;
It has begun.
The voice of God speaks redemption;
It has begun.
The voice of God speaks peace to the blighted masses of Southeast Asia;

To those whose every day is living death, the voice of
    God speaks peace.
From the sands of Iba,
It has begun.
Hallelujah!

                    Byrd Brunemeier, FEBC Engineer

    The Republic of the Philippines embodies a group of seven thousand islands located where the Pacific Ocean meets the China Sea. The Republic comprises fifty-seven provinces strung throughout this "Pearl of the Orient Seas." The sixty million inhabitants of the twelve-hundred-mile elongated string of islands are of diverse language groups. From the mountainous rice terraces of northern Luzon, where primitive Ifugao and other tribal people dwell, to the southern Philippines, whose Muslim Moro population seeks independence as a nation, they vary in size and cultural patterns.

    The great Muslim area of the Philippines is located in the south central and eastern section of Mindanao. The opportunity to build the first of FEBC's provincial radio stations came at Marbel on Mindanao. DXKI, Marbel, was the forerunner of eight such stations that were built in other strategic areas. They are Legaspi City, located in southern Luzon; Cebu City and Bacolod City, in the central Visayas; Davao, Zamboanga and Marbel on Mindanao; Iba, in northern Luzon; and a Mangyan tribal station on Mindoro in conjunction with Overseas Missionary Fellowship. All these stations are broadcasting in local dialects and are managed and staffed almost entirely by dedicated Filipino Christians.

    When the first provincial station at Marbel went on the air in 1965, the Maguindanaon tribal language was among the local dialects in use. After the station was on the air for a while, a delegation of colorfully dressed Maguindanaon people came down the mountain to visit the station. Their story was remarkable.

Fourteen years before, a pastor from the Marbel area traveled for several days through the jungle trails to their tribal village. He gave them the gospel message in the few days that he had stayed. Upon leaving he promised to return. But the thought of the rigorous jungle journey on foot and the mosquitos and leeches that had clung to his legs along the tangled jungle trail troubled him. He kept delaying the return he had promised so long before.

But now he reached them by radio. And the Maguindanaons listened in their jungle homes and recognized his voice after fourteen years! They traveled to the radio station to find the pastor. He assured them that he would soon return. Meanwhile they listened on their radios.

For many years FEBC has offered numerous Bible correspondence courses targeted toward winning and discipling new converts to Christ. The oldest course, The Bible School of the Air, started by veteran missionary Cyril Brooks in the early 1950's has passed the two-and-a-half-million enrollment mark.

There are several evangelical Bible schools and training centers in the Philippines where young people can prepare for Christian leadership in the churches and for foreign missionary endeavor. But the need for more trained leadership is great.

Dr. Dale Golding and his wife, Belvah, have served the Lord with FEBC for over thirty years. Dale prepares and produces a radio correspondence course on a seminary level. Its purpose is to train young men who desire to serve God, but who are financially unable to attend a Bible school or seminary; and to give a helpful teaching ministry to those faithful

Filipino pastors who need encouragement in their church ministries.

The Biblical Education for All through Media (BEAM) student enrollment presently numbers over seventeen hundred, an encouraging response for the short time it has been on the air. This seminary course entails an enormous amount of preparation for the on-the-air facet of the ministry as well as corresponding with the students and grading their lessons. But it produces rewarding results and makes a useful contribution toward the advancement of the church in the Philippines.

FEBC's Bocaue site houses a forty-thousand-watt AM mediumwave transmitter for DZAS, the local service for Metro-Manila. The daytime signal reaches eight million people in the Filipino language. At night the signal travels farther north and south covering over half of the sixty million people of the Philippines. Bocaue is also the primary overseas site for Southeast Asia.

Meanwhile, at Christian Radio City Manila (CRCM), the production center houses thirteen studios, including a large music recording studio where many of the programs are prepared and aired for the daily schedule. One can stroll down the hallways, looking in studio windows, and see individuals of different nationalities producing programs for release to their countries.

A master control in the production center is computerized and automatically controls programs from ten of the studios in the building simultaneously. This computer "brain" directs the programs to the Philippine domestic transmitters or to ten overseas transmitters, all within a 125-mile radius of Manila. Located at these overseas sites are forty-, fifty-, and 100-thousand watt shortwave transmitters and a 250-thousand-watt mediumwave transmitter. The system was designed by FEBC digital engineer, Marinus Landman.

Every ten seconds, the computer brain will give the engineer on duty an audio report of what is going on in each studio. He hears a voice on the monitor speak in Chinese; ten seconds later it may be Russian; another ten seconds may produce Burmese, Vietnamese, Indonesian, or any one of the languages being sent to the transmitters that are beamed to a country at that time. On the wall behind the computer control is a large map of the world. Digital light beams sweep across the map indicating the areas of the world that are being reached by Far East Broadcasting Company.

Programs in a transmitting schedule are normally fifteen or thirty minutes long, sometimes shorter. Whenever a program change is made in the schedule, the computer brain determines which transmitter and antenna system to send it to at the precise moment the new transmission begins. The schedule from Far East Broadcasting Company, Philippines is in seventy-one languages and dialects beamed to all the countries of Asia.

10

Penetrating the Bamboo Curtain

The phone in the Bowman house rang at 7:00 A.M. on June 3, 1989. Bob picked it up.

"Dr. Bowman, we've got to do something!" The Chinese-accented voice spoke with obvious fear and agitation. The speaker had been a young Communist Red Guard during China's Cultural Revolution, but he had found Christ through Far East Broadcasting Company's ministry to China.

He continued, "I received a telephone call from a friend in Beijing at two o'clock this morning. The People's Liberation Army is poised to strike the students at Tienanmen Square. There is going to be a terrible massacre! The Communists are showing their true face now."

Bob wired the news to the White House fruitlessly. A few hours passed and the Beijing government imposed an information blackout.

A month before the Tienanmen Square events climaxed, the Hong-Kong-based Chinese program staff of FEBC had responded with adjustments in their program schedule. They provided objective reports of the events at Tienanmen Square directly to FEBC's transmitters as they happened. Programs of comfort, condolences, biblical teachings, and Christian viewpoints on the issues were broadcast.

Second Corinthians 7:6 says, "Nevertheless God, who comforts the downcast, comforted us by the coming of Titus." Could it be that FEBC was the "Titus" sent by God to China in their deep affliction?

Beijing's official report indicated that no one was killed at Tienanmen Square. Research centers in Hong Kong reported that several thousand were murdered. The wounded, many of whom died in the hospitals, numbered more than ten thousand.

"China has not been closed to the gospel!" Bob Bowman stated emphatically. "God simply changed His method of reaching China with the gospel from the ground to the air." But somehow the majority of Christians in the West have not heard.

On October 1, 1949, Mao Tse-tung had swung the bamboo curtain closed. Communication with the rest of the world ceased for thirty long years. In the first months, self-accusation meetings were implemented in China. Christian was turned against Christian, friend against friend, and family member against family member. Missionaries were forced to leave. The Christian world turned sadly away, leaving only heartbroken missionaries and a few indomitable warriors of the faith to keep the prayer vigil for China.

But God is never taken by surprise. Before access was blocked, radio stations were being built on a safe perimeter. The first transmissions to China from Far East Broadcasting Company, Philippines, started on July 29, 1949. The People's Republic of China, headed by the Chinese Communist party, took control two months later.

Remembering the history of China through past centuries, the Chinese Communist party faced a problem. No central government had ever maintained complete control over the large nation, the main reason being lack of rapid communications with all the provinces and the people.

Immediately upon assuming power, the Communists began to build electronics factories in various parts of China. By 1972 eighty percent of the Chinese homes had at least one radio. The electronics factories were built for their own propaganda purposes, but God turned their use to His glory. Over the past forty-one years, radio has been God's primary method of communicating with the believers in China and furthering the task of evangelizing China's 1.2 billion people.

During the first years of the Communist dictatorship, before writing to the outside world was forbidden, letters from many of China's provinces arrived at Far East Broadcasting Company's address in Hong Kong. The Chinese heard the broadcasts in their own language.

David Morken, a missionary evangelist, was in Shanghai awaiting repatriation to America in 1950. He wrote to FEBC: "I wish I could adequately tell you how I feel about the work of Far East Broadcasting Company, as I listen to the well planned, professionally produced Christian programs coming from Christian Radio City Manila."

The Communists began closing the churches as well as compelling the missionaries to leave China. They forbade the people to write to foreign countries. But the letters FEBC had already received provided evidence that the radio signals were effective. During the thirty years from 1949 to 1978, each smuggled letter and word that came to FEBC by way of escapees was held like a precious jewel.

During many of those years the searching questions were: Do the people have radios—and if so, how many? Does the government allow them to listen to FEBC? Full answers were not easy to obtain. Faith kept the broadcasts going during those uncertain years.

During the Cultural Revolution when the Chinese postal system was not well controlled, some letters slipped out. Then, as censorship tightened again, the frequency of mail tapered off. FEBC kept a ten-year vigil of broadcasting to China even when there was little reply.

FEBC was often referred to by China's official press as an "enemy station." While China's government was attempting to eliminate God, FEBC was transmitting His Word to the Chinese people daily around the clock. It was dangerous for them to listen to foreign broadcasts. Some were listening secretly under blankets. It was even more dangerous to communicate with the stations. Those who were caught suffered large fines or prison terms. There were reports that some died for listening.

Yet some were willing to risk their lives to write. Some spent more than a day's wages for a stamp. However, FEBC, knowing the danger, did not encourage communication during those years.

In late 1978 when China's bamboo curtain cracked open slightly, a stream of thousands of letters poured into FEBC's Hong Kong office. By Western standards, only one in a thousand listeners will write to a radio station. In China many are not able to read or write. Many listeners are rural peasants who cannot afford a stamp or find writing materials or even locate a post office. The personal danger of writing is a strong deterrent.

FEBC estimates its China audience in the millions. To date, FEBC has received over a hundred thousand letters from every province and autonomous region of China.

When China first accepted outside visitors again, a Christian tour guide said that many young Chinese clustered around him and his group in the six major cities they visited. They inquired if he and his tourist friends were Christians. When he answered affirmatively, they said, "We are Christians too." When asked how they heard the gospel, they replied, "Through *Liang Yu Dentai*."

Liang Yu Dentai (Radio Friendship) is the name by

which Far East Broadcasting Company is known in China. The Chinese listeners often think the transmissions come from Hong Kong instead of the Philippines, Saipan, or South Korea because a Hong Kong mailing address is given on the air.

In 1949 there were 936 thousand evangelical believers in China. Reseach organizations are attempting to estimate the number of Christians there today. They have agreed that the number of believers in China now surpasses fifty million. Some think it is much higher.

Dr. Donald McGavran, church growth authority at Fuller Theological Seminary, noted the phenomenal growth of the number of believers in China. He observed that this took place when there were no missionaries, no Bibles, and no churches. Many pastors were dead or in prison, and it was dangerous for Christians to communicate the gospel on a personal level. Dr. McGavran wrote to FEBC: "Without doubt the majority of these new believers have come because of the broadcasts you have been sending to China. The whole Body of Christ owes Far East Broadcasting Company a debt of gratitude."

God has seen that the seed of the Word has been sown over all of China for the past forty-one years. In six major Chinese language and dialects, 375 thousand hours of gospel broadcasting were beamed in from FEBC Philippines, South Korea, and Saipan. The "Bible at Dictation Speed" program constantly supplied Bibles for those who could quickly jot down the Scripture.

A recent visitor to China told Bob of meeting a Christian who proudly showed him a well worn Chinese Bible. It was completely handwritten and sewn together, page by tattered page. The Chinese man said he had copied it down over the years, listening to *Liang Yu Dentai*'s "Bible at Dictation Speed" program.

The visitor said, "I wanted with all my heart to buy that Bible from him to give to you, but I could not bring myself to ask for such a precious possession."

Persecution beyond belief came in the years leading to the infamous decade called the Cultural Revolution which began in 1966. Censorship was severe. The young Red Guard, dedicated to Mao, rampaged through the countryside targeting intellectuals, teachers, Christians, and Buddhists. They burned Bibles and hymnbooks and desecrated the churches. Many high-ranking officers were thrown in prison or killed. Fighting between pro-Mao and anti-Mao forces stalled economic production and disrupted provincial governments.

Shortly after the Cultural Revolution began in 1966, letters to FEBC increased to six to eight per month. The letters that did slip out were written cautiously. The writers addressed the FEBC Chinese staff as though they were relatives. They never mentioned a radio station, though some referred to the "calling voice of God." They spoke of God's presence in the midst of persecution. Most letters concluded with one word: "Emmanuel" which means "God with us." Now and then a refugee brought out a letter. An occasional letter telling of a conversion encouraged the FEBC staff: " I have never tasted what love is before. Life was empty and uncertain. In 1971 I bought a radio and became a regular listener. I found the answers that have puzzled me for years. Therefore I decided to trust in God."

Thousands of people tried to escape. A Hong Kong police report said that only one in every forty who tried the swim to freedom succeeded. The odds against them were overwhelming. Capture by Communist gunboats, fatigue, starvation, sharks, and drowning in the cold water took their toll.

A letter to the Hong Kong office put it starkly: "Many

bodies float down the river, killed by these devils. Please remember in prayer those who want to escape."

A young man who had been the number three Red Guard leader in Shanghai, survived the grueling long swim in freezing waters to Hong Kong. While serving in a labor farm in China he came to faith in Christ listening to *Liang Yu Dentai*.

Stories of the persecutions and sufferings poured out of China. An aged grandmother escaped into the Portuguese Crown Colony of Macau. When the Communists took over her city, before her escape, they dug up the bones of missionaries, long buried in the graveyard. They grotesquely paraded the bones through her village for all the people to mock.

A young Chinese named Chen told of his grandfather:

> My grandfather first suffered persecution in the 1950s. He used the Bible openly but did not do much witnessing to other people. During the Cultural Revolution the young people of the Red Guard marched into our hometown and grabbed my grandfather. They saw the small cross he wore around his neck. They snatched it away from him and left.
>
> When they returned, they had made a heavy, large cross, which they hung around his neck. They displayed him to the people and mocked, "This is a Christian!" Then they burned all my grandfather's books. He had many kinds of books. Some he had gotten from my forefathers.
>
> My grandfather never cried before because he was a strong man. But when they burned his books and his Bible, he cried. He told me, "Chen, my faith was strengthened by the persecution."

Radio continued to be the major means of encouragement to the persecuted Christians. It provided hope to millions of listeners. Letters that slipped through the censorship expressed appreciation to the broadcasting staff whose voices they knew so well. The broadcasters had become old friends to these listeners during their time of fear and isolation.

The Communist government continued to prohibit listening to foreign broadcasts. Warnings in the press against the "enemy station" served as good publicity for FEBC. The people eagerly searched for the station they learned was prohibited. News of the gospel broadcasts spread by word of mouth. In spite of the danger they wrote, "We are listening in secret."

By this stage of the Cultural Revolution, the Red Guard was completely out of control. Mao called out the People's Liberation Army, and they sent over twelve million young people to labor farms. The Cultural Revolution wound down, and so did the trust the young people held in their once-revered leader, Mao.

Disillusionment reigned. Previously Mao had sent the young Red Guards through the countryside to destroy "old things." Now they were enslaved on farms doing hard labor for the rest of their lives. Hope for education vanished. They became interested in learning English to help them to escape to Hong Kong. FEBC taught English and the Bible was the textbook. With obvious intentions toward his future, one young person wrote: "I hope you can help me buy some books such as *Journey to the West*. My English improves a great deal through your English programs."

The Cultural Revolution came to an end in 1976. By then letters were telling of secret home meetings of believers. Some were openly worshiping in these "house churches": "In our hometown we have formed the church again even though we have not gotten the church building back. We hold the church in our home. And now we are asking the government to give the building back. Maybe someday they will."

A new relationship with China began as a result of President Nixon's visit in 1972. The wheels of diplomacy grind slowly, and seven years later the bamboo curtain parted slightly again.

The volume of mail to FEBC from China began to increase slowly at first and then more rapidly. In March 1979, 3,071 letters arrived in a single month. Many bore messages indicating that the writers had been listening for a long time and were only now able to let the broadcasters know that they had found faith in Jesus Christ through the broadcasts.

Since 1979 FEBC has received thousands of letters from house churches. Many of these churches were formed by people who found faith in Christ listening beside their radios. Their spiritual lives have been deepened by the teaching of the Word over the air. Personal contacts with families from China allowed FEBC personnel to understand more fully the tragedies of the years when Communists killed sixty million Chinese.

Mrs. Hsiao, an elderly American citizen, went to China as a missionary in 1923. She married there and raised a family. When the persecutions started, her husband, a Chinese Salvation Army worker, was taken to prison. She cared for her family under difficult circumstances, finding strength in listening to *Liang Yu Dentai*. After many years her husband died in prison, and her children were grown.

Restrictive conditions eased a little, and Mrs. Hsiao requested permission to leave China. Through the efforts of several friends, she received a visa. Arriving in the United States, she immediately made contact with FEBC.

Then she wanted permission from the China government for her children to join her in America. Her eldest son, Paul, a college professor, had suffered solitary confinement in a darkened, shower-sized cell for months at a time. Eventually he was allowed to join his mother. Annie Grace, his sister, had spent fifteen years in prison. She was punished for writing a letter of protest when her pastor was taken to prison. Just one month after her release, she arrived in the United States followed by her widowed sister and children.

In the years since 1979 many have believed that China's intent was to have better relations with the rest of the world. Indications showed that the leaders accepted the idea that Christians were valuable to the country. Western business investments in the economic structure helped China to double the national average income of the Chinese people in a ten-year period. Sadly, the massacre at Tienanmen Square set China back many years economically and dashed the young people's hopes for a democracy in the near future.

Two and one-half months before Tienanmen Square, on March 20, 1989, an astonishingly positive article was published by the famous Communist *Beijing Review News Magazine*. It acknowledged the mass move toward the gospel of Christ in an article titled "The Surge in China's Christianity." Several interesting reasons for the "surge" were given:

- China's religious history is deeply rooted in the past.
- Children of Chinese Christians almost always become Christians.
- They seek help from God to overcome physical illness.
- They seek Him to have their sins forgiven.
- They seek God out of loneliness.
- The people are in search of emotional fulfillment.

Though rapidly expanding production has helped the Chinese people to reach material aspirations, it does nothing to fill a spiritual void. The article concludes with one other reason for this unprecedented move toward God: the work of religious groups based overseas broadcasting Chinese-language gospel programs around the clock. This is a remarkable admission by the Beijing Press!

The surge of Christianity to which the official media of China refers brought an increase in believers of fifty times what it was in 1949. Four basic factors can be seen that resulted in this mass movement toward Christ.

Unceasing prayer for China: Missionaries who were forced to leave the land of their calling prayed fervently.

The witness of a small group of believers: About half of the 936 thousand believers in China became martyrs for Christ's sake at a time when personal witness was difficult. Their self-sacrifice made deep impressions on unbelievers.

Sowing the Word in God's perfect timing: Two months before the persecutions began, FEBC's broadcasts went on the air to China and have continued for forty-one years. The seed is sown in six Chinese languages. Over several transmitters, forty-two hours of broadcasting reach China daily.

The motivating force of the Holy Spirit: He has taken the three major reasons and has established a Church, in some respects like the one of the first century, against which the gates of hell could not prevail.

Dr. Dick Hillis, a missionary with the China Inland Mission (OMF), lived in China before and through the first days of the communist takeover. He is the founder of Overseas Crusades. In a letter to Bob and Eleanor Bowman, he wrote:

When you sent your first broadcasts into China, it was my privilege to hear them coming through in beautiful Mandarin, and I was thrilled. Thank you for forty-one years of faithfully broadcasting the Word. That vision and faith, though born small, has grown to the honor of God, to the defeat of Satan, to the building up and equipping of the saints, to the reaching of the lost.

The government that took over China, the country with the largest population in the world, in 1949 was not only hostile to the Church; it was determined to wipe out the Church. One of the primary reasons that Christians were able to stand firm and not yield to the demands of the government to throw away their faith was the fact that Far East Broadcasting Company was daily feeding them on the Word of God at dictation speed. Although they had lost their Bibles, they were not only able to hear but to copy the Word of Life. It was this faithful delivering of the message through radio that enabled the Church not only simply to survive, but to witness and grow. The story is miraculous. Some of the outstanding missiologists of our day consider the survival and growth of the Church in China to be one of the greatest miracles since Pentecost. To God be the glory!

The Word of God that you have faithfully sent out has been used by the Spirit to help believers to persevere in persecution and to be faithful unto death. The story of Far East Broadcasting Company is simply another chapter in the Book of Acts.

As the Lord protected and blessed His Church during the terrible persecutions of the Roman Caesars in the first centuries, so He keeps His promise today and continues to build His Church in the twenty-first century. One of His most powerful methods is the radio voice of FEBC.

We, who had to leave China at the order of the Communists, will forever thank God that the Church survived and grew because it was being daily fed by the Word of God through FEBC's broadcasting into that land.

Your Fellow Servants,
Dick and Ruth Hillis

11

Russian Love Letters

"Why are you getting all this mail from Russia?" asked a worker in the La Mirada, California, post office one morning.

Jack Koziol, FEBC Russian broadcasting department director, replied, "I decided to put the address: P.O. Box 1, La Mirada, CA 90637, on my broadcasts to the Soviet Union. Until the '*Glasnost* window' opened, I used overseas addresses for Russian people to write. Then their mail could avoid the strict censorship that had existed for four decades."

Excitement ran high at FEBC the memorable day when the first letter from the USSR arrived in Box 1. The number increased until there were 519 received in a single day and 4,840 in one month.

When Jack arrived at the La Mirada post office laden with packages addressed to people in the Soviet Union, more questions were asked. He replied, "We are sending Bibles to the people in the USSR."

"Where do you get their addresses?"

Jack said, "The people who write to FEBC from Russia request Bibles and give their return addresses. In my office I have a map with tiny colored pins clearly showing the multitude of cities and country villages across Russia from where letters are continually received. After nine months of marking these locations, I found no more room to place pins in the populated areas of the Soviet Union."

"Have most of the people who write always been Christians?" asked one postal worker.

"Not necessarily. We read of many who hear our broadcasts and become Christians. Thirty percent of the letters come from Russians who identify themselves as former Marxists, Communists, or atheists, who are searching for the truth. The letters speak eloquently of the gnawing spiritual hunger of the Russian people for God's Word."

When the conversation ended, the postal workers offered to contribute money to send more Bibles to Russia.

Glasnost is the Russian word for the current, more relaxed state of affairs between the USSR and the countries of the West. Since the *Glasnost* window opened, FEBC has sent over a hundred thousand Bibles, New Testaments, Gospels of John, and Bible commentaries through the mail in answer to these requests.

The decades preceding *Glasnost* were filled with suffering, imprisonment, even torture for those who corresponded with a Christian radio broadcasting company. One letter received from Siberia a few months prior to *Glasnost* was carried from the north of Siberia to Moscow, and there it was mailed with a prayer. The prayer was answered. FEBC received the letter:

> I started listening to FEBC broadcasts from Manila in the early 1960s. I came to faith in Christ and wrote to Manila asking for literature. FEBC responded with the requested material, but the package was confiscated by officials at the post office. I was seized by the KGB and sent to a psycho-prison where I remained for the past twenty years.

I wrote two other letters and a post card to FEBC since my release, but I did not receive a reply. I could wait no longer to say, "Hello respected brothers in Christ." Much I dare not share about myself. I was an electrician. I became a believer. Then misfortune happened. So, after twenty years I am now in freedom but afraid that I will be taken again. I suffer waves of doubt, fear of martyrdom, and no hope of deliverance from the repeated torture. But I keep saying to myself, "God will help."

The former prisoner's fourth attempt to contact the radio station was successful—an indication that *Glasnost* is working.

Many letters to FEBC from the USSR are presently indicating that *Glasnost* is in force. Some tell one story; some, another. One thing seems sure—Bibles and literature now sent to the Soviet Union are getting through. The following are short excerpts from some of the recent "love letters" that reached FEBC from the Soviet Union:

At this time there is not persecution of the believers. We Christians are very grateful to our leader General Secretary M. C. Gorbachev for this freedom. Also, we thank God because we can hear the gospel over the radio and, for you, even greater gratitude because of your great service to us. Indeed this is the fulfillment of the New Testament in Revelation 14:6: "Then I saw another angel flying in the midst of heaven, having the everlasting gospel to preach to those who dwell on the earth—to every nation, tribe, tongue, and people."

Another letter states, "While in prison I preached to criminals, and ten men were converted to the Lord."

And still another one says, "I have waited for sixty years to hold a Bible in my hands."

Glasnost appears to the Western world to be helping believers to worship more freely.

"How has *Glasnost* affected Christians in psycho-prisons in the Soviet Union?" is a question often asked today. One can only pray that freedom has been resurrected from the grave in which it was deeply buried within the USSR. So long as there is a single Christian in prison for his faith in Jesus Christ, be it a psycho-prison or a part of the Gulag that Solzhenitsyn has so graphically described in his writings, the freedom of the Russian people is not complete.

One letter to Jack Koziol read:

> Hello dear friend and colleague. Yes, I can call you "dear friend" because you are a friend to thousands of people who listen to your programs and find true grace in them. I call you "colleague" because I am a radio journalist now. I have been in the newspaper communication, not a short time.
>
> So, dear Jacob Fedotovich, between us is a great space. We do not know one another. I think of you as a close, sincere instructor, as a preacher showing the way leading us to the Light. You will say, "Only God shows people the way to the Light and to grace." But the Word of God came to us from your mouth. You broadcast from those stations which support and strengthen our spirits.
>
> Now, in order to come to this place in my life, it was providential for me to sit down at my radio and to find your wave. Truths, which were alien to me not too long ago, now go deep into my heart.
>
> I was a propagandist and an agitator. I was a Komsomol (Young Communist League) leader. I did many things in order to persuade young people that God doesn't exist and that Jesus is fiction. I taught them in study groups of Marxist-Leninist theory.

But when I listened to your programs, I began to understand that Christianity teaches us to be honest, good, and just. I heard your words about God's miracles, your prayer for those who had not found Jesus as Savior. Frankly speaking, your words went deep into my soul. From that time I began to listen to every program from Saipan. Every one of them helped me. Your voice reached into my heart.

And as a result, I repented before the Lord God and called Jesus Christ to be my Savior. On January 25 I was baptized in our Orthodox church. I am from a Jewish family. Can you understand how difficult that was for me? I will never renounce my newfound way. I praise our Lord Jesus Christ.

Christians in the West have difficulty understanding how much the radio broadcasts have advanced the gospel of Christ in the Soviet Union. Vera Koziol told of a time when she and Jack were in Siberia to meet Russian believers:

We needed directions to a church, so we approached a young man who was a vacationing school teacher from Mongolia. He graciously offered to show us the way. While we walked, he told us that his parents, though not Christians, had suffered terribly at the hands of the Communists.

We found the church, an old wooden building with a heavy fence around it, at the bottom of a hill. A dim light shone through the window.

When Jack knocked on the gate, the teacher looked around cautiously, not knowing what to expect. A thin, elderly man came to the gate and invited us into the courtyard. Jack gave his Russian radio name.

The man said, "Yes, I am well acquainted with that name." He took Jack in his arms and embraced him with deep emotion.

Jack turned to the schoolteacher friend and explained who he was and why he had come to the Soviet Union. The teacher seemed nervous; he had never been in a church before and wondered if he should enter. We assured him of the open invitation, but he asked to be excused, since he had seen us safely there. We exchanged addresses, and he vanished.

By this time, the pastor's wife rushed toward us. With great excitement she asked, "Is it true that the Russian broadcaster is here? Oh, come and have a meal with us."

As we ate, we cried and shared with quiet voices. The room was dim and the curtains were drawn. The pastor told us of people who came to their church asking for baptism, and he questioned them about how they heard the gospel.

"By radio," they replied. Some traveled fifteen hundred miles to receive a Bible.

The pastor also told us of many groups in remote places who listened to and appreciated the broadcasts. Often one member of a family would discover the gospel programs, accept the Lord, and then invite others to listen. A group of listeners dependent entirely upon the radio programs for spiritual strength, would be formed.

The pastor's wife said, "It's unbelievable! We just heard you on the radio. It is as though an angel of the Lord arrived, as though Jesus came to visit us!"

It is estimated that there are 39,750 isolated radio churches like the one the pastor mentioned to Jack and Vera. The names of gospel broadcasters like Jack Koziol, Rudi Wiens, Earl Poysti, John Sergei, and many others are household words across the Soviet Union because of their years of radio ministry to Russia. FEBC broadcasts the gospel twenty-two hours daily to the USSR from transmitters in the Philippines, South Korea, Saipan, and San Francisco. An estimated 1.59 million Russians have become believers through the isolated radio churches.

A Jewish woman discovered the broadcasts one morning between the hours of two and five. She wanted desperately to hear more, but she did not own an alarm clock. She asked God to awaken her, which He did each morning at that hour.

Soon she received Jesus Christ as her Savior. As she continued listening, she craved fellowship with other Christians, but she knew of none in her Siberian town. She prayed about it. That very night she heard the broadcaster say, "If you have no church and no believers in your area, seek out another lady and pray with her."

That morning at the marketplace, she eagerly scanned the faces of the people. Approaching a clerk in a stall, she asked, "Do you believe that God exists?"

To her astonishment the woman replied, "How dare you ask such a question! Of course God exists. I have a neighbor who is a Christian."

The clerk went home that evening and told her neighbor of the incident. The following morning, someone knocked on the Jewish woman's door and said, "I am a believer."

After a moment's hesitation the Jewish woman replied, "I am also a believer."

The visitor stepped inside, embraced her, and said, "Let's pray together."

A bond of Christian fellowship formed, and after a time the new Jewish believer was invited to a secret house meeting with other Christians.

On the other hand, one young Christian stated that the atheists in the Soviet Union have been given an advantage by the Communist government.

The atheists have an abundance of literature, TV programs, radio broadcasts, and much money to spend on influencing the minds of people. We were taught with much persuasion in school that God does not exist. Therefore, in our society, especially for young people, it is difficult to openly express one's faith. To believe in God one must cross the barriers of mockery; to believe in God, one must disregard the opinions of people.

Near the end of another letter from a Russian listener:

How well I recall the day in 1950 when we heard your broadcast for the first time. We surrounded the radio receiver and prayed and rejoiced as we listened to programs from Manila.

Many Nicodemuses are listening in secret, desiring to hear the Word of God. With much love I close this letter to you.

From Our Family,
Greetings in Christ

Glasnost seems to be making a radical change in the Soviet Union. Perhaps it is because so many "Nicodemuses" desire to hear the gospel today and are listening.

12

Radio Peradache

"**D**uring our times of difficulty, the monks here received great blessing through 'Radio Peradache.' I want to thank you on behalf of us all," said the black-robed monk as he stood in the courtyard silhouetted by ornate towers and golden onion-shaped domes.

The words of the neatly bearded monk stunned his listeners. They were unsolicited, unexpected, and filled with significance. His black eyes had been remote and expressionless while he conducted the tour of the cathedrals, palaces, and refectories comprising the complex of the Trinity Monastery of Saint Sergius. Now his expression softened at the moment of recognition. The American visitors from Far East Broadcasting Company realized how the spoken Word of God, quietly heard by international radio in the private moments of these monks' lives, had nourished their souls.

The Trinity Monastery of Saint Sergius is located seventy kilometers northeast of Moscow in the city of Zagorsk. Bob and Eleanor Bowman, Jack and Vera Koziol, and Tim Koziol were among the 700 thousand visitors who see these historical buildings annually.

As they walked through the halls, they were awed by the antiquity and lavish expressions of divine devotion of the past that had been allowed to survive the great Russian revolution. In 1920 Lenin proclaimed the Trinity Monastery of Saint Sergius to be a state museum of history and art. Today, Russians proudly display the churches as unexcelled examples of medieval art, culture, and architecture. The monks of Saint Sergius became curators and guides, living without their holy Scriptures, forbidden to conduct Mass. Their contact with true worship became Radio Peradache, the FEBC Russian broadcasts.

In May 1989 Pastor Logvinenko, president of the Russian All-Union Evangelical Christian Baptists (AUECB), and Reverend Commandante, a pastor from Kiev, visited the United States headquarters office of Far East Broadcasting Company in La Mirada, California, and spent time with the president, Bob Bowman, and the Russian program director, Jack Koziol. All of the protestant churches in Russia were organized under the AUECB. Although they were called Baptists, the organization included evangelicals and all denominations.

President Logvinenko extended an invitation to visit the Soviet Union as guests of the churches. He said, "You will see what your radio broadcasts have done in the Soviet Union. You will meet the people who listen."

Late in August the official invitation came. It was extended to Mr. and Mrs. Bowman, Mr. and Mrs. Koziol, and Timothy Koziol, who would go as a photographer. An automobile and driver would be provided, and the guests would be free to travel wherever they wished. All expenses would be paid by the churches in the Soviet Union. The hospitality would include visits to places of present and historic interest as well as church meetings and visits with church leaders. The first sightseeing expedition was the imperative visit to Red Square and Lenin's tomb in Moscow.

Sergey, who had driven the van to pick them up at the

Moscow airport the night before, gathered the five and their guide, Pastor Volodya, at their hotel beside the Moskva River. Volodya was appointed by the AUECB to be their host for the entire trip. He was quiet, but his personality radiated Christian love.

A youth pastor, Sergey was tall and husky with smooth white skin and red cheeks. His curly black hair reached almost to his heavily muscled shoulders. On his black leather jacket was the American/Russian friendship pin.

"He has been chosen as our driver because of his strength," Vera whispered. "He can protect visitors from any hooligans they might encounter."

It was a short drive to the entrance of the famous Red Square. Sergey drove the van up on the cobblestones and parked at an angle outside the gates. Hundreds of Russians and foreigners lined the vast cobblestone-paved square leading to the Lenin shrine.

Sergey frowned when he saw the long wait to visit Lenin's tomb. He jumped out of the car and dashed through the lines to the guardhouse.

Soon he ran back to the parked van and started rummaging through the cubbyhole (glove compartment). His black eyes shone with delight as he pulled out some books and rushed back to the guardhouse.

Volodya explained, "Sergey told the two soldiers that he has a party of Christians from America who are on a tight schedule. They did not have time to wait in the long lines. Could a place be found up front for them?"

"All right," one guard had said, "but first you must give us two Gospels of John."

No wonder Sergey smiled broadly! Was this really Russia, where suppression of anything religious had been mandatory for decades? Here in Red Square beside the Kremlin, the most sacred of all Communist monuments, the Gospel of

John opened the way for five American Christians to view the body of the only object of reverence allowed by the Soviet Government.

Interestingly, Stalin used to lie in state beside Lenin. Fifty million people were killed during the Stalin era. Wave after wave of officials around Stalin who knew too much were murdered. After Stalin's contribution to Russian history was reevaluated, his body was taken out and buried beside the Kremlin wall. There Stalin awaits the day when he will be tried by the Russian courts and convicted of the repugnant deeds that he committed against his own people. His body will be dug up and destroyed "by the people."

Although this was the first view of the famous square for the Bowmans, Bob remarked later that it seemed strangely familiar. How often on television he had watched the thousands of workers and soldiers marching in patriotic pageantry across its vast cobblestone expanse along with an ominous display of rockets, tanks, and new inventions of war.

Escorted to a place near the head of the lines, they faced the rolling red-brick walls of the Kremlin where the entrance to Lenin's tomb protruded beneath. Looking up at the Kremlin wall, Bob imagined the uniformed members of the proletariat raising their hands in salute to a passing parade below.

Towering behind the American visitors was the strange castlelike architecture of GUM. Moscow's largest department store. At the far end of the Square rose the fantastic cluster of wooden spires and onion-shaped domes of Saint Basil's Cathedral. Its overornate gingerbread, painted in bright and contrasting colors, seemed to totter between the grotesque and the sublime.

Near the tomb, restrictive reverence was demanded, compelling absolute silence. Visitors, men and women, were brusquely requested to button their coats and jackets.

As they walked up the granite steps and then down the dimly lit stairway inside, repeated strains of melancholic music accompanied them. Entombed inside and glowing in soft light was Lenin's body. It lay in mysterious preservation like an ancient pharaoh.

Then the Americans walked past the tombs of fallen heroes, away from the sound of the mournful music, and away from the oppressive feeling imparted by the grim guards. Standing there in the sunshine, they turned their conversation to the love of the living Christ.

The next stop for the American visitors was the Moscow Baptist Church, and a dinner planned by President Logvinenko of the AUECB. When the Communist government took control of Russia, all protestant denominations (Presbyterian, Evangelicals, Lutheran, Pentecostal, Mennonite, Baptist, and others) were placed under one name: Baptist.

The Moscow Baptist Church was the only protestant church in the entire city of Moscow that the Soviet government allowed to stay open. Billy Graham and other evangelists had stood in its pulpit, but worshipers had been discouraged and sometimes forcibly prevented from contacting them personally.

For decades children and young people were harassed and barred by the government from entering this church. Nevertheless the faithful, mostly "babushkas" or grandmothers, crowded its walls in worship. Now as the van turned down a narrow street, a plain white building with an unimposing entrance came into view.

Inside the Americans met with thirty-four ministers who came from Siberia, the Ukraine, and across the eleven time zones of the USSR. This was a first meeting for these pastors who gathered to discuss and pray about the opportunities the new "freedoms" promised. They wanted to discuss ways to implement these freedoms to evangelize the nation. They surrounded Bob and Jack, eagerly relating what Christian radio had done in each part of Russia.

All were ushered into a large sunlit room where they crowded around tables laden with great platters of sliced jellied meats *(kholadets),* sliced salamis, cheeses, pickles, dark and light bread, and butter. Plates were filled with fresh tomatoes and cucumbers covered with sour cream, meat dumplings *(p̃iroghki),* and cabbage rolls *(goulubtzy).* Tall glasses of pink fruit drink *(kompote)* and large pitchers for refill were also on each table.

When the first course was consumed, beaming church women brought in steaming bowls of meaty cabbage soup *(shchi).* Dessert was thin pancakes *(blini)* served with sour cream, syrup, and tall glasses of hot tea.

The visiting pastors and American guests were introduced. The fellowship was exuberant, crossing over the language barriers. They discussed how the government seemed to be allowing more concern for religious freedom than ever before. The laws were not changed, but four freedoms were being exercised without hindrance: freedom to propagate the gospel, freedom to train young people and children in the churches, freedom for churches to own property, and freedom to travel around the country without the former restrictions.

After dinner, everyone walked through the old, narrow hallway into the sanctuary of the famous church. It was filled to capacity, but room was reserved for Eleanor, Vera, and Tim in the high balcony. Jack and Bob were escorted to the platform.

The high-ceilinged sanctuary was long and narrow. Painted white and pale gray, it was ringed on three sides by high balconies filled with worshipers and foreign visitors. The choir, largely composed of young adults, was in the center balcony. A wide carpeted aisle leading to the front divided the crowded main floor. Behind the tapestry-covered altar decorated with vases of flowers, Bob and Jack sat with other pastors. Behind them were several narrow stained-glass windows.

The service lasted about three hours. The program was filled with lovely hymns by the choir and congregational singing, interspersed with messages and recitations of poetry. Children, ages four to eight, occupied the front rows. They listened intently without giggling or talking to one another.

When President Logvinenko introduced Jack Koziol as Jacob Fedotovich Kozlov (the way he is known on the FEBC broadcasts), a low murmur spread through the congregation. The Russian believers strained to look at this man they had listened to for thirty-two years.

Bob spoke first and Jack interpreted. They told the story of God at work in the FEBC ministry—how it was founded, and so on. Bob said, "God is making these broadcasts possible to Russia and many other nations through loving Christians in the West who earnestly pray and generously give of their offerings."

These Russian believers had often wondered how it was done, and they felt overwhelmed by such love.

When Bob asked how many in the congregation listened to the broadcasts, knowing smiles crossed their faces. And when he asked for a show of hands, practically everyone in the audience raised a hand.

Then it was Jack's turn to preach a message in his native Russian. While Jack ministered to the Moscow congregation, a lump formed in his throat, and he constantly fought back tears. The congregation responded to this man of God. Now and then the sound of sobbing could be heard as people held handkerchiefs to their eyes and wiped away tears.

The hunger for the Word of God was incredible. In closing, Jack mentioned that he had his *Question and Answer Book* available for those who wished a copy. He explained that it was printed in answer to the many questions the Soviet radio listeners asked in their letters. There was a stampede to the front.

After the service the group journeyed for ten hours in a sleeper compartment bound for the Ukraine and Kiev. They were met in Kiev by Reverend Commandante, who had accompanied President Logvinenko to the FEBC office the previous May. The large city of Kiev, capitol of the Ukraine, is one of the oldest in Eastern Europe. Called the "Garden City," the third largest metropolis in the Soviet Union spreads its green landscape on both sides of the Dnieper River. Expansive park lands surround awe-inspiring monuments.

On the way to the hotel the driver of the van told stories concerning the radio ministry. He told of a schoolteacher who gave poor grades to his Christian students and ridiculed them. Then the man became ill and was confined at home for a time. During his illness he began listening to his radio and found Radio Peradache. When he heard a message on repentance, he received Christ. Upon returning to school, he apologized to his students and asked their forgiveness.

The driver told another story of a teacher who taught atheism. One day he bought a Bible so he could find the errors in it. He studied it for ten years and was converted. Scripture came alive to him.

Early Sunday morning Bob and the group waited for the driver outside their hotel, which faced a huge Lenin memorial. The streets filled with people strolling in twos or threes, escaping from the overcrowded apartments for some space and privacy.

A comfortable van, provided by the local Christian leaders, soon picked up the group of American visitors. They drove past large monuments and museums, past endless tall apartment buildings. Soon green countryside opened up, bordered by thick forests.

Small wooden cottages lined the dirt roads. Some of these homes were one hundred years old; some, only decades. Each was painted a bright color with white or contrasting hues on the wooden jigsaw gingerbread around the windows and eaves. The bright paint, now faded to soft pastels, spoke of the severe winters the boards had weathered.

These had been spared the ruthless bulldozing imposed by the government. Most small homes had been destroyed when the Communists drove the people to the crowded city apartments where they could control them more easily.

Turning another corner, the van stopped in front of some country homes. A small path led down between wooden fences entwined with vines and rosebushes. It led to the House of Prayer, built with love by the Russian believers. The church was hidden discreetly behind the small homes.

The Sunday morning congregation gathered around. Some were still arriving, walking down the country lanes to the church. An eighty-seven-year-old babushka stopped to talk. Her bright yellow head scarf was tied firmly under her chin. All married women wore scarves in the church services.

The grandmother greeted the American visitors: "The gospel is going into all the world, thankful to radio." She spoke joyously in Russian, and Jack translated. She kissed Eleanor in the customary greeting of the Russian believers.

"Oh, the suffering." She shook her head in sorrowful remembrance as pain etched her face. "During the days of Stalin, I was hunted down by the secret police and driven from my home for being a believer. My children stood inside the house peering fearfully out the windows. I saw them sobbing as I was dragged away.

"I pleaded with my captors to let me go to them, but

they would not listen. I was taken to the mines to work in water up to my hips.

"Ah, the suffering. God gives the world warning. He will judge the world. God is faithful." Then she fell silent. How could she convey to Western Christians the extent of the years the Russian believers had suffered for their faith?

As with all the churches visited by the Far East Broadcasting group, this one was filled. Beautiful young children dressed in bright colors lined the balconies and front rows. Starched white pom-poms adorned the heads of many of the little girls. They sat up straight and attentive, yet happily childlike.

The high windows of the small but beautifully built church let in the morning sunshine. Joyous, reverent worship and praise lifted in glorious sound.

Bob described his feelings during the service: "The early morning sun shone brightly through a huge window on the east side of the church. I felt it symbolized the new light that seems to be shining on the believers in Russia."

After the service the pastor said to them, "The radio broadcasts are very important. Many are saved while listening to their radios. Others are spiritually prepared by the radio broadcasts and come to church and accept Christ. And many who listen are too old and too far away from the church to attend the services. Some of our young people await the day when they will be able to go out as missionaries."

Though the Russian people rejoiced in the new freedoms they enjoyed, the visitors questioned how long these would last. In the meantime the Russian believers intended to make every moment of their present freedom count.

The Bowmans and Koziols traveled to Minsk and Brest, visiting ten churches in all before returning to Moscow. Stories of conversion and evidence of a wide listenership to

FEBC emerged wherever the group went. They heard of high government officials who had come to Christ. Believers claimed there was a revival across the country. Russians thought the new freedoms enjoyed were caused by President Reagan's influence on President Gorbachev. And they had heard that Gorbachev had said that he expects the church to bring peace to the land.

Across the Soviet Union the American visitors asked the questions, "How many listen to the FEBC broadcasts? How many listen to Radio Peradache?" The answer was the same. Practically every hand in the audience went up each time. They realized that millions of Russians listen to Christian radio.

In the Moscow hotel the last evening Bob checked Far East Broadcasting Company's radio signals from Saipan shortwave and South Korea mediumwave and found them coming in loud and clear. He listened to FEBC Saipan for three and one-half hours of prime time, six to nine-thirty in the evening. The signal was steady throughout that period.

As their plane took off for home the following morning, new snow of late autumn began to fall on Moscow. Bob looked at his friend and coworker and thought of the important part Jack had played for thirty-two years in broadcasting the gospel to the USSR.

CHAPTER

13

The Message in
Their Own Tongue

One afternoon when Bob Bowman walked down the hallway of Far East Broadcasting Company international headquarters to the studios, he saw Chong Lee, Hmong broadcaster to the Laos mountain areas. Suddenly Bob remembered a story that a Christian and Missionary Alliance missionary, Ed Gustafson, had told him over thirty years before when they met in Hong Kong. Ed had worked among the Hmong and Lao people and had cooperated with FEBC in preparing programs in these languages for fifteen years.

Ed told Bob a story about a Hmong group high in the mountains of Laos. The people of the area listened to Manila programs in their own language, and they decided to become followers of Jesus Christ. The announcer on the radio said to write to Box 3, Vientiane, for further information. But there was a problem. No one in the village could write!

In conference with their chief, a delegation was sent to the post office in Vientiane to find out who owned Box 3. They first made contact with a post office clerk who put them in touch with the wrong people. They met someone who returned to their village with them and started working among them. But soon the Hmong recognized that the message they were now being taught was not the same as they had heard on the radio.

Again they sent a delegation down to the post office in Vientiane. This time they were able to contact the post office director who happened to be the secretary of C & MA for the National Church of Laos. He informed their missionaries, and they accompanied the delegation on the return journey into the mountains—a journey of six days on foot.

The chief called the Hmong of the area to a meeting to consider the message they had heard on the radio. The culture of the area was community based. When the chief discussed the matter with his people, the entire group became Christians. Bob related this incident to Chong Lee as they stood in the hallway.

"Chong Lee, when you lived in Laos, did you ever hear a story like that?"

A smile crossed Chong Lee's face.

"Dr. Bowman, that was my village. I was eight years old when those events took place."

"Chong Lee, tell me, how many of your villagers came to faith in Christ at that time?"

"Over three thousand."

The FEBC staff had no knowledge that Chong Lee's conversion dated back to his boyhood in that Hmong village until that day in the hallway at La Mirada!

Chong Lee has been the ministering voice from FEBC to his mountain people for ten years. He receives as many as seventy-seven letters in a single week from his listeners, though the writers place themselves in jeopardy by writing.

Since FEBC began broadcasting in Asia in 1948, the airwaves have become saturated with broadcast signals. The listener has multiple choices. As his hand twists the radio dial, it stops when he hears a message with words he understands and to which he can instantly relate.

When a program in one of the 120 languages fills the airwaves, it can find many expatriate listeners living in surprising parts of the world—Russians in Australia and South America, Koreans in China, Vietnamese in many countries, and Chinese all over the world. Also, large groups of homesick contract workers, stationed for years in countries far from home, eagerly listen when they discover a program in their own tongue.

A Christian national, giving the good news of the gospel in his native tongue, speaks in the culture and thinking of the people. He avoids the pitfalls of local prejudices and taboos and knows almost instinctively how to reach the hearts of his own people.

A Chinese doctor aboard a merchant ship plying the East China Sea first heard the gospel in his own language, but spoken by a foreigner. After his conversion he said:

> The Western broadcaster spoke my beloved Mandarin so atrociously that I kept tuning in time after time. It irritated me and intrigued me as to why he was trying so hard. Finally the message got to me and I accepted the Lord. I vowed that if I ever had the opportunity, I would gladly broadcast the gospel.

Eventually, this doctor prepared medical programs in Mandarin in FEBC's Hong Kong studios.

His reference was to a missionary who had lived in China for decades before the Communists came. His message before the microphone in Manila was given with earnestness—sometimes with tears. He loved the Chinese people. The Holy Spirit will often take that kind of love and translate imperfect words by His power to convey a message.

But these are exceptions.

FEBC is often asked: How do you get the many programs to feed thirty-two transmitters three hundred program hours a day in 120 different languages? Each language requires a continuity of messages to keep the daily broadcast schedule going. The logistics are exceedingly complex and ingenious.

Far East Broadcasting Company has recording centers in many parts of the world. Ninety percent of the staff members are citizens of the country to which they broadcast. Their programs are produced in their own mother tongue—the Chinese Christian speaking to the Chinese, the Indian to the Indian, the Russian to the Russian, and so on through the 120 language groups.

In addition to the offices and studios owned and operated by FEBC, hundreds of others are operated by world evangelism organizations in cooperation with FEBC.

In these recording studios the message of Jesus Christ is taped in the language and culture of each environment, using the finest pastors, teachers, evangelists, and ethnic music of that country. These program tapes are sent in a steady stream from the recording studios to the transmitter sites and beamed back to their country daily. The mail that program draws, written in the local languages, is received at the local recording center and usually answered there.

The preeminent operational discipline of the organization is programming. The general program director of FEBC is Frank Gray, a native of the United Kingdom. Frank served with the British voluntary service overseas in Laos where he gained an interest in foreign missions. It was in Laos that he met his wife Henny, a native of Holland. When many missionaries and national Christians were forced to leave Indochina in the mid-1970s, Frank came to the United States and became attached to the FEBC Indochinese programming department in 1979. In 1980 Frank was appointed general program director of FEBC-USA. He and Henny have been stationed in Manila since 1982.

Jim and Cynthia Bowman have been with FEBC for twenty-six years. As a child, Jim spent years in the Philippines with his parents, Bob and Eleanor. Jim was drawn to the ministry while he was a student at Fuller Theological Seminary. Because of his fluency in Spanish, he first served FEBC at KGEI. He is now the director of field operations.

The operational policy of the organization has always been to focus on the basics of the evangelical message and to present the gospel of Jesus Christ in a way that will say to the world in truth: Christ is not divided. We are one in Him. Each broadcaster, whether on staff or from cooperating organizations, may present a message with utmost scriptural liberty. Yet according to the governing policies, it must be done in a way that will not reflect adversely upon the beliefs or practices of any other cooperating entity.

The language center in Bangkok, Thailand, was first built in 1969 for program production in the Thai language. Manila Overseas broadcasts are heard in Thailand, and time is also purchased on many local Thai commercial stations, which cover the major portion of the country.

As many as three thousand responses come each month from Thai listeners. They are followed up with Bible correspondence courses. Many have become Christians from among the mainly Buddhist population. New converts are channeled into the local churches. Apichai Branjerdporn, director of the Thailand production center, received the following letter:

> I've wanted to write to you for a long time, but I didn't have money for stamps. You don't know how much we appreciate your broadcast. We have no other hope, so people are tuning to your Christian station."

Hachiro Kobayashi, who was an insurance executive and former pastor, now directs the Tokyo, Japan, office and recording studio. The nightly broadcasts through FEBC's Cheju-do station in South Korea's Yellow Sea are making an impact on the young people of Japan. Keiko Yoshazaki, administrative assistant to the director, shows Christian love for the spiritual needs of the people of her country. She received the following letter from a listener: "I am in a dilemma! I do want to become a Christian and confess my sin, but it will bother my parents. Please guide me." Another listener shared his need: "I was led to Christ through FEBC. But my faith has fallen asleep! Please continue to 'lead me' so that I will grow to be a better disciple for Jesus."

The twelve studios at Christian Radio City Manila are program sources for the local and overseas transmitting stations at Manila, Bocaue, and Iba. Stations in Legaspi, Cebu, Iba, Bacolod, Zamboanga, Davao, Mindoro, and Marbel serve the local provinces in their own dialects.

The FEBC Indonesian Office and Recording Center (YASKI) in Djakarta is directed by Samuel Tirtamihardja. The thirty Indonesian Christian staff members minister to a varied Indonesian audience throughout the more than 13,600 islands.

Indonesia's many states are held together by ocean, and much of their interstate travel is by water. Commerce of the county is largely by sea. Interisland boats and commercial ships at sea are an important segment of the international radio audience.

Many sailors with difficult problems have been helped through listening. One seaman explained that he had some inadequacies that filled him with "doubt and imbalance." He confessed to "promiscuous ways" in which he had committed sin.

But he called himself a Christian, though he had never really lived "in a Christian way," as he put it. The programs produced by the Djakarta staff influenced him. Changes occurred. The Holy Spirit brought conviction. And he wrote:

> Now I understand and realize who I am. I want to turn away from sin and come to the Righteous Way that is the Lord Jesus Christ. As I sail the oceans on board a ship, I often listen to your radio programs. They have shown me how to overcome my life's problems. I am a faithful listener of the "Father of Comfort" program. Through it God's glory has shown in my life. I hope you will counsel me in spiritual matters so that I can grow in faith.

Hong Kong has been the main Chinese language center for FEBC since 1957. Directed by Ken Lo, a staff of fifty-five Chinese prepare suitable programs for one billion people. Programs recorded in Hong Kong provide a spiritual lifeline to those over the border—those who described themselves as being "in a wilderness without hope."

In 1997 the Crown Colony will return to the authority of China. That year holds a dilemma for the Hong Kong production center. The Chinese government has stated that no religious organization involved in ministry that is influencing religion in China will be allowed to remain in Hong Kong. FEBC will stay there as long as God allows, but meanwhile other Chinese production centers are being built away from Hong Kong.

The Singapore recording center is directed by Dr. David Chen, Overseas Missionary Fellowship, and is the base of another Chinese radio production center. Letters like this one from a listener in Hebei Province, China, make laboring for His kingdom worthwhile:

> Our church was formed through listening to your broadcasts. However, we are very young spiritually and

there are no pastors in our midst. Please pray that the Lord will raise up His servant to take over His flock. Thank you for your concern and your ministry to us.

Vancouver, British Columbia, is the headquarters of FEBA/Canada. For many years, this FEBC associate office has provided prayer, financial assistance, and personnel support. It is also a language production center that tapes Chinese and other language programs.

When Hong Kong returns to China, these alternate major Chinese production centers will enable the continuation of the extensive forty-two hours of the daily Chinese language schedule to China. Reverend Philip Leung, who was the assistant to the director in Hong Kong, came to Canada as director of the Chinese language studios.

Toronto, Canada, has a large Chinese population, increased daily by those emigrating from Asian countries. Most speak Mandarin Chinese, and a production studio has been set up there.

The newest branch office and Chinese production studio of Far East Broadcasting Company is located in Monterey Park, California. John Lin, who has directed FEBC Okinawa, Hong Kong, and Singapore over the past twenty-eight years has accepted this new challenge with his wife, Florence. It will be a communication and support outreach with the large Chinese population in the Los Angeles area and across the United States.

La Mirada, California, is the international headquarters of Far East Broadcasting Company. General administrative coordination of FEBC worldwide operations takes place here. Daily four recording studios produce tapes by Russians, Vietnamese, Cambodians, Laotians, and Hmong for the overseas transmitters. San Hay Seng, the only Cambodian pastor to escape Cambodia when it fell, ministers to his home country. Inta Chanthavongsouk directs the Laotian broadcasting to Laos.

Burma is a country of intrigue—a land of Buddhism and pagodas. In 1951 FEBC began its first broadcasts to Burma where a staff of Burmese Christians now operate a recording studio and a follow-up office. The director is Ronnie Tin Maung Tun. In a "Bible-Read-Along" program, a Burmese Bible was offered to those requesting it. Over ten thousand letters arrived in response. Ninety percent of the writers were Buddhists; among them were Buddhist priests.

Thousands of letters reach the Rangoon office each month. Following is the story of Sai Lwin, a twenty-year-old Shan tribesman. His overpowering ambition was to be rich. He left high school early to become a trader along the Thai-Burma border. His work was dangerous.

One day the young Burmese encountered robbers along the highway and a shoot-out followed. Several young workers traveling with Sai Lwin were killed. Sai Lwin was left badly injured. He begged the robbers to kill him, and then he fainted.

Some days later he regained consciousness in a hospital in the city of Taunggyi, completely blind, not knowing how he got to the hospital. He was aware that his hopes of riches were at an end. He would be a burden to his family. The following months, while still in the hospital, he tried suicide several times. When he returned home, he continued seeking ways to end his life. Living had become unbearable. However, he wrote to the Rangoon office that hope came in an unexpected manner: "One day, I heard your radio message in Burmese. It said, 'Come unto Me, all you that are heavily laden, and I will give you rest.' Even though I didn't fully understand the whole message of salvation, there was a strange sense of peace in my heart." Sai Lwin continued to listen and wrote: "I committed my life to Christ and became an entirely new person. I used to feel remorse about my mishap. But now I realize how gracious God is to save me and to make me His own son."

Missionaries are no longer allowed to work among the fifty million people in Burma. The door closed in 1966, making the radio ministry there even more valuable.

On one occasion Bob Bowman visited Rangoon, Burma. He traveled up the Irrawaddy River to visit the village of some ardent listeners who invited children into their home to hear the daily FEBC broadcasts.

When the boat arrived at the village dock, Bob was taken by horse and buggy to the home of the Burmese listeners. Outside the house stood sixty children with placards welcoming him to their village. These were Hindu children, most of whom had come to faith in Christ. They proudly showed him notebooks, copiously filled with daily notes written during the broadcasts.

During the noon meal an English program aired from Manila. Bob Bowman was the speaker. The children looked puzzled. How could this man be on the radio in Manila and in their small village at the same time?

14

Eyes Beyond the Horizon

"I memorized the entire New Testament." A twenty-year-old Chinese girl spoke these words halfway around the world from her home. The astounded audience consisted of a small group of Bible college students from Asian countries, who gathered regularly for Bible study and prayer.

Ashook Singh, a young student from India, told Bob Bowman the story:

> When our Asian prayer fellowship gathered to share the Word of God, I noticed that Tracy Tan seldom opened her Bible. Yet she never missed a word when she quoted Scripture.
>
> One day I said to her, "I have also memorized Scripture but not so much! How could you do that?"
>
> She replied, "When we were in China, we heard a broadcast from FEBC in Manila called 'The Bible at Dictation Speed.' They read and I wrote.
>
> "Sometimes we burned the papers afterwards. If we felt threatened, we swallowed the evidence. But we memorized the verses before destroying them. In that way I memorized the whole New Testament."

The program "Bible at Dictation Speed" has been aired over FEBC for more than thirty-five years. An announcer reads a short phrase from the Bible while a second individual copies it down in Chinese characters, making sure enough time is allowed. These programs are usually only fifteen minutes long, and the Bible is read slowly.

A special story showing the results of the Holy Spirit working in Indonesia, a country of many islands, is about a young Muslim named Hadi. His sister first began to listen to FEBC Manila in secret by using an earphone with her transistor radio. After a year she became a Christian.

She convinced Hadi that he should listen. In a matter of months he too accepted Christ as his personal Savior. His father learned of this and beat Hadi until he was lying in a pool of blood on the floor of their home. The mother and grandmother intervened. Hadi left home and became a wanderer on the streets of Djakarta.

Hadi kept contact with his five brothers and eventually led them all to Jesus. He worked and saved enough money to attend Bible school in Djakarta and there became a young preacher. His youngest brother became ill and was placed in a hospital. At first the parents refused to see their son because of his conversion to Christianity. When told he was dying, they relented. With his last breath the young son pleaded with his Muslim parents to receive Jesus Christ. They did. The son dropped his head on a pillow and died.

Hadi told the story to Bob Bowman when visiting the La Mirada office one day in 1986. Hadi and his sister had first come to Christ more than thirty years before. He is now pastoring a church in Indonesia.

Another dramatic example of unimagined results of broadcasting came to Bob Bowman's attention while he was in London. At the close of a meeting a handsome twenty-two-year-old man approached him and said, "You don't know me, but I am in the London Bible College today, studying for the ministry because of Far East Broadcasting Company."

Although some mail is received regularly at the Manila stations from shortwave listeners in Great Britain and Western European countries, this part of the world is not FEBC's primary target objective. Bob looked at the man with a puzzled expression.

The young man continued, "I was in government work in Borneo, living far from God. My job was to do survey work among the tribal people." He paused and smiled. "I was young and expendable, so I was sent to work among the headhunter tribes, deep in the interior.

In this remote jungle, several days' journey from civilization up twisting dangerous rivers, I felt like I stepped backward into another age. When the tribespeople met me, they became strangely excited. I found extraordinary coincidences that led me into a bizarre experience.

My Anglo-Saxon name had the exact sound of the name of their heathen god, and their ancient legends told them that their god had light hair. Since I was blond, they were convinced that a descendant of their god had entered their midst. In superstitious reverence, they began to worship me.

At first I considered this harmless. It amused me. But as boredom and the strangeness of the primitive life gripped me, I began to encourage the idea.

Unfortunately, my companion in the research, a young Australian, was affected adversely. The jungle life, the loneliness, and the unreal relationship with the people oppressed his mind, and as time passed he lost his reason completely to the point of violence.

I tied him in the boat to keep him from throwing himself into the crocodile-infested water, and we traveled five days by river to civilization and medical help. When I returned alone to my outpost, I was shaken and sobered. It was then that I began to listen constantly to a transistor radio that a Chinese rubber trader, who came up the river annually, had used to pay for his rubber.

In listening to the Manila FEBC transmissions night after night, I came face-to-face with Jesus Christ. My whole life was changed, and today I am preparing for the ministry.

The medium of broadcasting is not limited by geographical or political boundaries. Radio is one of the few "missionaries" today capable of taking the gospel to the "ends of the earth." Radio is intimate and personal. Programmers are able to reach across great distances to meet with listeners at their private locations.

Another interesting story of Christian broadcasts reaching an unlikely place involves a young man named Bill Aguerra. A person meeting him would never suspect he had committed murder three times. He was one of the many prisoners on Bilibid's death row in the Philippines, led to faith through the prison ministry of Olga Robertson who placed PMs among those on death row.

Filipinos are considered the musicians of the Orient, and they play stringed instruments in the lilting Filipino style. Far East Broadcasting Company began the Papuri annual praise concert many years ago in the Philippines. The purpose was to encourage young Christian Filipinos to develop a hymnology typical of their own culture.

For the concert, hymns written by the local Christian musicians are judged by a music committee headed by the esteemed Professor Pajaro, a Christian at the University of the Philippines. The winning seventeen songs, sung by Filipino Christian artists and groups, form the program for the Papuri concert each year.

As a result, many new Christian songs are now being sung in the Philippine churches. And these young Filipinos are changing the sound of the provincial broadcasting stations which FEBC operates through the country.

Young Bill Aguerra, on death row in Bilibid prison, heard of the Papuri hymn-writing competition over FEBC's local radio station DZAS. He wrote the story of his own conversion in hymn form and was one of the top winners.

Far East Broadcasting Company petitioned the president of the Philippines to allow Bill to leave death row for the evening to sing his own composition. It seemed an impossible request, but at the last moment Bill was paroled to FEBC for the evening. He arrived under armed guard.

The lights dimmed. Barefooted and dressed in yellow prison garb, Bill walked on stage with his guitar, sat on the edge of a stool, and began to strum. In his plaintive but beautiful voice he sang the story of his own conversion to Jesus Christ. He picked up the tempo of the chorus in a moving way that proclaimed, "But I have been born again."

The spirit of the crowd was with him as he moved toward the climax: "Though I am confined in a prison cell, my spirit is free."

At that point the young prisoner from death row broke down in tears, and the entire audience wept with him.

Christ's final words to His disciples show the purpose of the work of FEBC: "Go therefore and make disciples of all the nations, baptizing them in the name of the Father and of the Son and of the Holy Spirit, teaching them to observe all things that I have commanded you" (Matt. 28:19, 20a).

Radio recognizes no boundaries. It enters the homes, hearts, and ears of all Christians, irrespective of denomination. The broadcast media are accessible to secret believers, unbelievers, seekers, doubters, agnostics, and lastly but equally important, to those who may never otherwise hear the message of salvation.

Who are the people who listen to FEBC? What effect do the broadcasts have on them? The following illustrates a cross section of listeners showing the diverse national and societal groups and individuals who have heard and responded to the broadcasts.

- A Filipino student
- A headhunter from Sarawak
- A Sundanese tribesman from Indonesia
- A Buddhist monk in Sri Lanka
- A Thai farmer far up in the riverlands
- A fierce Moro of the southern Philippines
- A Hong Kong merchant
- A lonely leper on Palawan
- A Brahman from Nepal
- A Japanese university student
- A plantation worker in Malaysia
- A Nagaland tribesman of eastern India
- A shipboard medical doctor on the China Sea
- An American GI in Manila
- A sailor in the Indian Ocean
- A former Russian atheist professor of physics
- An athlete from Moscow
- A Russian actress formerly on heroin
- The mayor of a Ukraine city, imprisoned
- An isolated radio church in Russia
- A house church in China
- A patient in a Korean hospital
- An Amharic listener in Ethiopia
- An isolated village pastor in Japan

- A young Christian in Vietnam
- A Muslim from Bangladesh
- A Cambodian refugee
- A young listener in Guatemala

And the list goes on almost endlessly, from the fifty-one thousand responses received by FEBC each month from listeners in nations around the world.

Far East Broadcasting Company is committed to providing all men, women, and children on earth the opportunity to turn on their radios and hear the gospel of Jesus Christ in languages they can understand. Then they can become followers of Christ and responsible members of His Church. "World by 2000" is the plan to complete this task in ten years with God's help. The method used is International Missionary Radio. There are 1.5 billion radios in the world today, one for every four people.

In 1985, the presidents of World Radio Missionary Fellowship (HCJB), Trans World Radio (TWR), and Far East Broadcasting Company (FEBC) met to discover ways to combine efforts in reaching the world with the gospel by radio. A few months later, Sudan Interior Mission International (SIMI) which operates Radio ELWA in Africa, joined the meetings for "World by 2000."

These four pioneer missionary radio entities, whose signals virtually cover the earth, now meet regularly at both the presidential and operational levels. Together they design strategies and make specific plans to reach areas of the earth that do not presently have any, or adequate, Christian broadcasts.

Radio in Church-planting Evangelism (RICE), developed by Frank Gray, FEBC general program director, is an important radio programming philosophy that plays a part in "World by 2000." Frank stated that RICE seeks to identify each specific group of people. It attempts to understand them in the context of their particular set of cultural, geographical, religious, socioeconomic, and linguistic parameters. Then it designs a radio strategy to move these people toward Christ and into the fellowship of His Church. RICE plants churches, trains pastors and lay leaders, and nurtures Christians among each group of people. A description of RICE has been printed by the Lausanne Committee for World Evangelization in their *Lausanne Occasional Papers.*

An interesting fact has come from the research done on the "World by 2000" project. Ninety-seven percent of the people of the world speak 276 major languages. These are "people groups" or nations of one million or more.

HCJB, TWR, ELWA, and FEBC presently broadcast in 184 languages, not all major languages. They need another 159 languages among them to attain the 276 languages spoken by 97 percent of the world's people. These organizations believe that, although it is an immense task, the goal can be reached as radio ministries, national churches, and missionary organizations cooperate to accomplish this vision.

The difficulty facing broadcasters is that the remaining 159 languages often represent areas of high resistance to the gospel. And they often have no significant Christian community from which to draw native speakers. Many of the areas, as in Indonesia, are Muslims and extremely hostile to Christianity. Another problem is that financial support is difficult to raise for some of these languages since they are obscure and remote from the supporting public in the West.

What lies in the future for Far East Broadcasting Company as it continues to lift its eyes beyond the horizon? Executive Vice-President John Yakligian explained that FEBC made the decision for a major expansion of the Bocaue, Philippines, overseas transmission facility. The initial portion of the project includes acquisition of more than fifty acres of additional land, a new transmitter building, a major electrical substation, four hi-tech/hi-gain antennas, and four 100-kilowatt transmitters. In a later phase, the building will be constructed to accommodate 250-kilowatt and 500-kilowatt units. The estimated cost of the project is $6 million. As throughout its history, Far East Broadcasting Company is looking to God to provide the funds for this essential project.

The Philippines is geographically the "hub" of East Asia. From this location, and within "easy coverage" of a fifteen-hundred-mile radius, lie Indonesia, Indochina, Malaysia, Thailand, Burma, and China. The population of these centers total 1.3 billion people.

FEBC's field operations director, Jim Bowman, said:

FEBC is committed to seeing its listeners reached by the gospel. One hundred and twenty languages and dialects, three hundred program hours a day, and thirty-two stations are meaningless statistics unless people find Christ through this vehicle. It is not enough to stand in a field and scatter seed. What matters is whether or not that seed is properly sown so that it may produce the prayed-for harvest.

Missionary Radio

This is not just the story of four decades of miracles and labor, of remembered and recorded history. This is the story of faith working in the present—faith ever unfolding, ever evolving, ever revealing ways to bring the message of the gospel to people everywhere.

Far East Broadcasting Company cannot stand on miracles of the past, nor can it be nourished by inherited blessings while the world is caught in a rushing torrent of change. Faith redesigns the methods, charts the future, and propels the activity around one immutable truth: the changeless Christ fills the intrinsic need in the hearts of individuals of all nations in every age.

Dipping into hidden valleys, circling thousands of remote islands, sweeping up inaccessible mountains, penetrating curtain barriers, entering the privacy of the home—this is missionary radio. Finding open hearts in the lonely byways or the teeming cities—this is the ministry of Far East Broadcasting Company.

The heart's need is always the same everywhere. Yet the presentation of the airborne message must capture the attention of the listener in his own language and reach his understanding. The gospel must not only storm the entrenchments of minds locked in primitive ignorance, but it must make inroads on the questing minds of the new generation of intellectuals and scientists produced by education. With the Lord leading the way, FEBC expands its ministry to move to the future as it lifts its eyes beyond the horizon.

Appendix

Statement of Faith

Far East Broadcasting Company is an extradenominational radio ministry enterprise for the sole purpose of taking the gospel of Christ to the world by radio. In so doing it seeks to cooperate with and support existing missionary efforts and the ministry of the greater body of Christ worldwide.

FEBC believes that the gospel radio ministry should present a united and consistent message for edification of others. Cooperation in such an enterprise as this may be achieved and maintained only by loyalty to a common and positive agreement in the broadcast message. In Christ we have fellowship with evangelical denominations and missionary groups, and we base our cooperation upon the following great truths of the Bible:

We believe:

The Bible to be the inspired, the only infallible, authoritative Word of God.

That there is one God, eternally existent in three persons: Father, Son, and Holy Spirit.

In the deity of Christ, in His virgin birth, in His sinless life, in His miracles, in His vicarious and atoning

death through His shed blood, in His bodily resurrection, in His ascension to the right hand of the
Father, and that He will personally return in power
and glory.

That for the salvation of lost and sinful man, regenera-
tion by the Holy Spirit is absolutely essential.

In the present ministry of the Holy Spirit, by whose in-
dwelling the Christian is enabled to live a godly
life.

In the resurrection of both the saved and the lost; they
that are saved unto the resurrection of life, and they
that are lost unto the resurrection of damnation.

In the spiritual unity of believers in Christ.

Geographical Scope of the Ministry

The radio ministry of Far East Broadcasting Company
daily covers geographical regions of the world where two-
thirds of the world's 5.1 billion people reside. Transmissions
are regularly beamed to Asia, Eastern Europe, the Middle and
Near East, East and South Africa, and all of Latin America.
Production studios are set up in various places throughout
the world to serve the transmission sites. Support offices provide both administrative and financial help.

FEBC/FEBA Operational and Support Offices

Country	Location(s)
Aruba	Oranjestad (Joint project with The Evangelical Alliance Mission)
Australia	Caringbah, NSW
Burma	Rangoon
Canada	Burnaby, B.C.; Toronto, Ont.
Hong Kong	Kowloon
India	New Delhi; Bangalore

Country	Location(s)
Indonesia	Djakarta
Japan	Tokyo
Kenya	Nairobi
Korea	Seoul; Inchon; Taejon; Cheju-do
Lebanon	Beirut
Netherlands	Zeist
New Zealand	Hamilton
Pakistan	Islamabad
Philippines	Manila; Iba; Bocaue; Legaspi; Cebu: Bacolod; Davao; Marbel; Zamboanga; Calapan; (Joint Project with Overseas Missionary Fellowship)
Saipan	Susupe; Marpi
Seychelles	Victoria
Singapore	Singapore
Thailand	Bangkok
United Kingdom	Worthing, Sussex
United States	La Mirada, California (Los Angeles area); Redwood City, California (San Francisco area)
Zimbabwe	Harare

Languages

FEBC/FEBA broadcasts in 120 languages and dialects. Large program blocks are devoted to major languages, such as Chinese and Russian, but significant program time has been dedicated to smaller language groups, especially Asian tribal peoples. Many of these groups have been identified as "unreached peoples" by the Lausanne Committee on World Evangelization.

Language	Country	Speakers (millions)
Achang	China	0.021
Akha	China	0.800
Aklanon	Philippines	0.350

Language	Country	Speakers (millions)
Alangan	Philippines	0.004
Amharic	Ethiopia	10.000
Amoy	China	10.001
Arabic	Middle East	80.000
Bahnar	Vietnam	0.085
Bicolano	Philippines	2.500
Bengali	Bangladesh	152.000
Bhojpuri	India	41.000
Blaan	Philippines	.100
Black Tai	Vietnam	0.250
Bru	Vietnam	0.093
Burmese	Burma	22.000
Byelorussian	U.S.S.R.	9.475
Cantonese	China	54.000
Cebuano	Philippines	10.263
Chamorro	Marianas (U.S.)	0.075
Chavacano	Philippines	0.280
Chin-Asho	Burma	0.100
Chin-Haka	Burma	0.085
Chin-Tidim	Burma	0.100
Chin-Falam	Burma	0.150
Chrau	Vietnam	0.020
Chru	Vietnam	0.020
Eastern Cham	Vietnam	0.050
English	Many Countries	403.000
Farsi	Iran	22.600
French	Several	109.000
German	Several	119.000
Hakka	China	42.800
Hanunoo	Philippines	0.007
Hindi	India	182.000
HRE	Vietnam	0.080
Halang	Vietnam	0.012
Hmong	Laos	0.250

Language	Country	Speakers (millions)
Ilocano	Philippines	5.500
Ilonggo	Philippines	4.000
Indonesian	Indonesia	7.000
Javanese	Indonesia	70.000
JEH	Vietnam	0.010
Jingpo	Burma	0.245
Jarai	Vietnam	0.163
Japanese	Japan	116.000
Kannada	India	25.000
Khmu	Laos	0.400
Khmer	Cambodia	7.758
Kirghiz	U.S.S.R.	2.000
Koho	Vietnam	0.100
Korean	N. & S. Korea	69.000
Karen-Pwo	Burma	1.270
Karen-Sgaw	Burma	1.300
Katu	Vietnam	0.030
Kuki	India	0.042
Kazakh	U.S.S.R.	7.600
Lao	Laos	3.000
Lahu	China	0.477
Lisu	China	0.524
Lushai	Burma	0.336
Malagasy	Malagasy	10.000
Malayalam	India	21.938
Mandarin	China	731.000
Marathi	India	50.000
Malay	Malaysia	17.500
Mnong	Vietnam	0.023
Meithei	India	1.100
Minangkabau	Indonesia	7.500
Mongolian, Chi.	China/Mongolia	3.500
Mundari	India	1.390
Muong	Vietnam	0.370

Language	Country	Speakers (millions)
Naga-Ao	India	0.075
Naga-Angami	India	0.044
Nepali	Nepal	16.000
Nung	Vietnam	0.100
Oromo	Ethiopia	4.700
Palaung, Pale	Burma	0.055
Pashto, Eastern	Pakistan	7.500
Polish	Poland	39.000
Portuguese	Brazil	154.000
Rawang	Burma	0.100
Rade	Vietnam	0.100
Raya	Philippines	0.008
Rengao	Vietnam	0.015
Roglai	Vietnam	0.025
Romanian	Romania	23.000
Russian	U.S.S.R.	154.000
Sambal Botolan	Philippines	0.032
Sambal Tina	Philippines	0.065
Sedang	Vietnam	0.040
Shanghainese	China	18.001
Shan	Burma	2.500
Sindhi	Pakistan	14.000
Sinhala	Sri Lanka	10.616
SAMAL	Philippines	0.100
Somali	Somalia	5.600
Sundanese	Indonesia	25.000
Spanish	Latin America	10.793
Stieng	Vietnam	0.048
Swatow	China	10.001
Swahili	Kenya	30.000
Tagalog	Philippines	10.019
Tamil	India	50.000
Tagabawa	Philippines	0.040
Tadyawan	Philippines	0.002

Language	Country	Speakers (millions)
Tboli	Philippines	0.080
Telugu	India	45.000
Thai	Thailand	20.000
Tho	Vietnam	2.000
Tausug	Philippines	0.492
Tawbuid	Philippines	0.006
Tibetan	China	4.000
Tigrinya	Ethiopia	4.000
Ukrainian	U.S.S.R.	45.000
Urdu	Pakistan	41.000
Varhadi-Nagpuri	India	6.390
Vietnamese	Vietnam	55.000
Wa	China	0.633
White Tai	Vietnam	0.100
Yakan	Philippines	0.060

Transmitter Locations

Transmitter	Location	Target Area	Power	Freq.
KGEI	San Francisco, CA	Latin America	50Kw	SW
KGEI	San Francisco, CA	Russia	250Kw	SW
KFBS (5)	Marpi, Saipan	Russia, China	500Kw	SW
KSAI	Susupe, Saipan	Saipan local	10Kw	936KHz
C-100	Iba, Philippines	Russia, China	100Kw	SW
Phil.OS (5)	Bocaue, Phil.	S.E. Asia, India	250Kw	SW
GF-100	Iba, Philippines	S.E. Asia	100Kw	SW
HLAZ	Cheju-do, Korea	Russia, China	250Kw	1566KHz
HLKX	Inchon, Korea	Korea, S. China	100Kw	1188KHz
HLAD	Taejon, Korea	Taejon local	3Kw	93.3MHz
DZAS	Bocaue, Phil.	Philippines	40Kw	702KHz
DZFE	Karuhatan, Phil.	Manila area	10Kw	98.7MHz
DWRF	Iba, Philippines	China	250Kw	1458KHz
DWRF	Iba, Philippines	Iba local	7Kw	1458KHz

Transmitter	Location	Target Area	Power	Freq.
DXAS	Zamboanga, Phil.	Zamboanga	5Kw	1116KHz
DXFE	Davao, Phil.	Davao local	5Kw	1197KHz
DXKI	Marbel, Phil.	Marbel local	5Kw	1062KHz
DYFR	Cebu, Phil.	Cebu local	3Kw	98.7MHz
DYVS	Bacolod, Phil.	Bacolod local	5Kw	1233KHz
DWAS	Legaspi, Phil.	Legaspi local	1Kw	1125KHz
DZB2	Calapan, Phil.	Mindoro	1Kw	3.8MHz
DZH6	Bocaue, Phil.	Philippines	15Kw	6.03MHz
FEBA (3)	Seychelles	Mid and Near East Africa, India	300Kw	SW

Far East Broadcasting Company is maintained by the gifts of individuals, churches, and organizations who believe that radio is a powerful means of communicating the gospel of Jesus Christ throughout the world. Frequently large donations are received, but it is the faithful smaller gifts of many that fund the Far East Broadcasting Company operations from month to month.

The Far East Broadcasting Company is a Charter Member of the Evangelical Council for Financial Accountability.

For further information, please write:
Far East Broadcasting Company
P.O. Box 1
La Mirada, CA 90637-0001

About the Authors

Eleanor G. Bowman is the wife of Dr. Robert H. Bowman, president of Far East Broadcasting Company. For twenty-three years she wrote, edited, and did the layout for the FEBC publications as well as designing the art work. Eleanor is an artist, with emphasis on portraits of Oriental faces. Eleanor, Bob, and their two sons lived in the Orient for several years. She has traveled overseas extensively with Bob, serving FEBC for over four decades.

Susan F. Titus is the associate director of the Biola University Writers Institute. She also serves as an advisory board member for the Orange County Writers Fellowship, a publishing consultant for Educational Ministries, and an advisory board member for the *Christian Communicator*. She is a frequent speaker at Christian writing conferences around the nation. Susan has authored four books and four leader's guides.